Globalisation, Regionalism and Economic Interdependence

How has increasing economic integration at the regional and global levels affected the functioning of the global economy? What are the consequences of globalisation and regionalism for world trade, production processes and domestic economies? What kind of economic adjustments do these phenomena imply in terms of factor mobility and relative costs?

Globalisation, Regionalism and Economic Interdependence addresses these and other questions by exploring the relationship between globalisation and regionalism from both academic and policy-making perspectives. It assesses the extent to which increased global and regional integration has changed the functioning of the world economy and analyses the implications for global trade, the relocation of production, structural changes and the international transmission of shocks. With contributions from both academics and professionals, this book is an invaluable guide to the increasingly important effects of the interaction between globalisation and various different forms of regional integration.

Filippo di Mauro is Head of the External Developments Division at the European Central Bank in Frankfurt. His first book was *The External Dimension of the Euro Area* (Cambridge, 2007), co-edited with Robert Anderton.

Stephane Dees is Principal Economist in the External Developments Division at the European Central Bank in Frankfurt.

Warwick J. McKibbin is Professor and Director of the Centre for Applied Macroeconomic Analysis in the ANU College of Business and Economics at the Australian National University, Canberra. He is also Professorial Fellow at the Lowy Institute for International Policy in Sydney and Non-resident Senior Fellow at the Brookings Institution in Washington, DC.

Globalisation, Regionalism and Economic Interdependence

Edited by

Filippo di Mauro,
Stephane Dees

and

Warwick J. McKibbin

CAMBRIDGE
UNIVERSITY PRESS

CAMBRIDGE UNIVERSITY PRESS
Cambridge, New York, Melbourne, Madrid, Cape Town, Singapore,
São Paulo, Delhi, Dubai, Tokyo, Mexico City

Cambridge University Press
The Edinburgh Building, Cambridge CB2 8RU, UK

Published in the United States of America by Cambridge University Press, New York

www.cambridge.org
Information on this title: www.cambridge.org/9780521182607

© Cambridge University Press 2008

First published 2008
First paperback edition 2010

A catalogue record for this publication is available from the British Library

Library of Congress Cataloguing in Publication data
Globalisation, regionalism, and economic interdependence / edited by
Filippo di Mauro, Stephane Dees, and Warwick McKibbin.
   p.   cm.
ISBN 978-0-521-88606-2
1. International economic integration. 2. Free trade. 3. Regionalism.
4. Globalization. I. Di Mauro, Filippo. II. Dees, Stephane. III. McKibbin,
Warwick J., 1957– IV. Title.
HF1418.5.G5735 2008
337–dc22

                                                          2008024828

ISBN 978-0-521-88606-2 Hardback
ISBN 978-0-521-18260-7 Paperback

Contents

Figures

Tables

Contributors

Robert Anderton is Adviser, External Developments Division, European Central Bank.

Prema-chandra Athukorala is Professor, Research School of Pacific and Asian Studies, Australian National University, Australia; Faculty of Economics and Finance, La Trobe University, Australia.

Matthieu Bussière is Economist, International Policy Analysis and Emerging Economies Division, European Central Bank.

Stephane Dees is Principal Economist, External Developments Division, European Central Bank.

Filippo di Mauro is Head of External Developments Division, European Central Bank.

Ingo Geishecker is Chair of Governance, University of Göttingen, Germany.

Holger Görg is Reader in International Economics, School of Economics, Research Fellow, Leverhulme Centre for Research on Globalisation and Economic Policy, University of Nottingham, United Kingdom.

Paul Hiebert is Principal Economist, Euro Area Macroeconomic Division, European Central Bank.

Warwick J. McKibbin is Professor and Director, Centre for Applied Macroeconomic Analysis, ANU College of Business and Economics, Australian National University, Australia; Professorial Fellow, the Lowy Institute for International Policy, Australia; Non-resident Senior Fellow, the Brookings Institution, United States; and Board Member, Reserve Bank of Australia, Australia.

Bernd Schnatz is Principal Economist, External Developments Division, European Central Bank.

Daria Taglioni is Economist, External Developments Division, European Central Bank.

Isabel Vansteenkiste is Economist, International Policy Analysis Division, European Central Bank.

Nobuaki Yamashita, Research School of Pacific and Asian Studies, Australian National University, Australia; Faculty of Economics and Finance, La Trobe University, Australia.

Preface

Jürgen Stark[1]

One of the main features of recent times has been the establishment of new major players in world markets amid the rapid diffusion of information technology. With emerging Asia, as well as central and eastern European countries, rapidly integrating in a more globalised economic setting, worldwide competition has sharpened, also leading to major changes in the structure of international trade. While globalisation was unfolding, regionalisation, another – possibly older – process was gaining momentum as well, most notably in Europe. How are these two processes interrelated, though? Are they complementing or contradicting each other?

To be sure, globalisation and regionalism are not mutually exclusive and cannot be seen in isolation from each other. Both encompass a strong increase in cross-border transactions in goods and services, capital, labour and natural resources. Both imply a dramatic change in the international transmission of shocks and in the ways that economies relate to their international environment. Both confer clear economic benefits, but there are also significant challenges to face.

At the ECB we are well aware of such issues, and in 2005, together with the Lowy Institute for International Policy and the Centre for Applied Macroeconomic Analysis at the Australian National University, we jointly organised the conference 'Globalisation and Regionalism'. Drawing partly from this conference, the book edited by di Mauro, Dees and McKibbin sets out to reply to the above-mentioned questions from both an academic and a policy-oriented viewpoint. Using a broad range of methodologies and techniques, the various chapters provide an overall understanding as to how the acceleration in the globalisation process interacts with the process of regional integration. The main aim is to analyse the implications for global trade, the relocation of production, structural changes and the international transmission of shocks.

---

[1] Member of the Executive Board of the European Central Bank (ECB).

Against the background of increasing economic integration at the global and regional levels, policies have an important role to play in order to improve economies' adaptability to new challenges, thereby raising the overall welfare of their citizens. From a euro area perspective, the Economic and Monetary Union (EMU) and the enlargement of the European Union (EU) – a prime example of regionalism – have not only fostered European economic integration but also made euro area countries better prepared for the challenges of globalisation. The euro, in addition to providing participating countries with a strong currency and a credible monetary policy, has helped them to cope with increasing trade and financial openness. The EMU has also heightened the need for other policies – beyond monetary policy – to be more proactive and coordinated. Interestingly, greater integration within Europe has gone hand in hand with stronger integration of Europe within the global economy. In trade terms, for example, the openness of the euro area as a whole – as measured by the share of total trade in GDP – continues to rise, and much more rapidly than for the United States and Japan, which shows that, despite increasing regional integration, there is no evidence that Europe is developing as a 'fortress'. Quite the contrary.

This notwithstanding, there is no space for complacency. While positive signs are evident, further adjustments appear to be needed to improve the functioning of the euro area economy. In particular, in several domains, the euro area still appears to be slow in adjusting to the major transformations occurring in its global and regional environment. Looking ahead, in the face of increasing trade liberalisation, protectionism and the shielding of jobs and industries from international competition are not conceivable as options. In order to reap the full benefits of globalisation, the euro area must make further efforts towards a knowledge-based economy. In this context, promoting firms' capacity for innovation and workers' skills are indeed crucial policy steps included in the Lisbon agenda. At the same time, economies need to adjust to the reallocation of production and the new competition from emerging markets in certain sectors. Economies with uncompetitive product markets and rigid labour markets not only fail to adjust to technological change but are also more vulnerable to shocks associated with the globalisation process. Reforming product and labour markets is therefore important to foster innovation and increase productivity potential, while raising the adaptability of all economic agents to a changing environment. In this respect, there is solid evidence that the euro area can turn this challenge into success for its citizens.

Introduction

Stephane Dees, Filippo di Mauro and
Warwick J. McKibbin[1]

Globalisation has implied a sharp abatement of barriers to economic exchanges between countries. In the immediate aftermath of World War II the process mainly involved advanced economies, but more recently it has increasingly included less advanced and transition economies, which by now are substantially integrated into the world economy. Global integration has also been accompanied by a sharp increase in regional trade agreements (RTAs), which constitute a logical means by which neighbouring countries may take up the challenges and opportunities implied by globalisation. The European Union is a prime example of regionalism. Today there exist more than 300 regional trade arrangements in the world, including free trade agreements (FTAs), customs unions and common markets. But how are globalisation and regionalism interconnected? Do they tend to complement each other as part of the same phenomenon or is there a tension between them? And, if the complementarity prevails, how do globalisation and regionalism affect the international transmission of shocks at a time of major structural changes? The main objective of this book is to address these issues, both theoretically and empirically.

Chapter 1 (International linkages in the context of global and regional integration, by Stephane Dees, Filippo di Mauro and Warwick J. McKibbin) gives an overview of our understanding of globalisation and regionalism and creates a unified and coherent overall perspective in which to situate all the various aspects covered by the different chapters. The first part of the chapter provides stylised facts regarding the globalisation process, the various regional integration experiences and the internationalisation of production processes. In the second part, various global models are used to evaluate how global and regional factors have changed

---

[1] Respectively Principal Economist, European Central Bank; Head of Division, European Central Bank; and Professor and Director, Centre for Applied Macroeconomic Analysis, ANU College of Business and Economics, Australian National University, Professional Fellow, the Lowy Institute for International Policy, and Non-resident Senior Fellow, the Brookings Institution.

across countries in the last few decades. Then, as globalisation and regionalism have made domestic economies more sensitive to global and regional developments, numerous adjustments have become necessary in the functioning of these economies, especially in terms of the allocation of resources and income. The final part of chapter 1 focuses on the impact that globalisation and regionalism have on labour and capital allocation, including income distribution and economic welfare.

Chapters 2, 3 and 4 focus on the impact of globalisation and regionalism on trade integration, product fragmentation, production relocation and firm performance.

The collapse of communism in central and eastern Europe, together with China's reform process towards a more market-based economy since the early 1990s, have been major factors fostering globalisation and triggering a significant reorientation of international trade flows. Using a gravity model, chapter 2 (Trade integration of the central and eastern European countries and China: has it reached potential?, by Matthieu Bussière and Bernd Schnatz) sheds light on the overall degree of trade intensity of a large number of countries as well as the depth of bilateral trade linkages with major economies. In particular, it assesses the trade integration of the central and eastern European countries (CEEC) and China into world markets. Overall, the gravity model indicates that the industrialised countries still tend to display above-average external trade intensity, while among emerging market economies it is mainly south-east Asian countries that exhibit high trade intensity. China – given its size and location – is also found to be rather well integrated into the world economy, while many of the CEEC are far less integrated.

The main new feature of the current upturn in globalisation is the associated changes in production processes, which have been greatly internationalised. Chapter 3 (Patterns and determinants of production fragmentation in world manufacturing trade, by Prema-chandra Athukorala and Nobuaki Yamashita) examines the implications of international production fragmentation for analysing global and regional trade patterns. It is found that, while 'fragmentation trade' has generally grown more rapidly than total world manufacturing trade, some disparity across regions is worth pointing out. In particular, the degree of dependence of east Asia on this new form of international specialisation is proportionately larger compared to North America and Europe. International production fragmentation has certainly played a pivotal role in continuing dynamism of the east Asian economies and their increasing intra-regional economic interdependence. There is, however, no evidence to suggest that international production fragmentation has contributed to lessening the region's dependence on the global economy. On the contrary, growth dynamism based on vertical specialisation depends inescapably on extra-regional trade in finished articles, and this dependence has in fact increased over the years. Overall, these results suggest that trade in components and trade in finally assembled goods have a very different nature and must be treated separately.

Increased outsourcing also provides a boost to the productivity of firms that outsource abroad some parts of their production process. Chapter 4 (Going global: trade, internationalisation of production and domestic performance of euro area firms, by Ingo Geishecker, Holger Görg and Daria Taglioni) investigates productivity differences between multinationals, exporters and purely domestic firms using firm-level data from the whole euro area. It analyses the extent to which euro area companies have internationalised their production in the period 1996–2004 and also discusses whether the internationalisation of the euro area economy has coincided with improved productivity and area-wide competitiveness, domestically as well as internationally. The chapter focuses on globalisation-induced firm selection effects (i.e. the exit of the least productive firms from the market) and share shifting effects (towards the most efficient firms). The linkages both to composition changes within industries and to changes in euro area aggregate economic performance are also studied. The chapter aims to highlight persistent patterns linking a firm's performance (particularly relating to its productivity) and its level of international engagement (non-exporter, exporter, foreign investor). It shows that firms that establish affiliates abroad are larger, more profitable and more productive than firms that do not. Moreover, there are performance premia (in size, profits and productivity) for multinationals with a large number of affiliates abroad relative to those with a small number.

Turning to how globalisation and regionalism affect the functioning of domestic economies, chapters 5 and 6 look at the cases of the euro area and the United States, respectively.

Chapter 5 (Globalisation and the trade channel in the euro area, by Robert Anderton and Filippo di Mauro) details how interaction between foreign shocks impacts on euro area domestic demand, underlining in particular the role of regional (intra-euro area trade) versus global forces. Since the late 1990s the strong performance of the global economy has appeared to find little correspondence in terms of euro area activity, casting doubts on the strength of the trade channel in the euro area – a puzzle, given the very open nature of the euro area, at least as far as its constituent economies are concerned. The chapter shows that the ultimate impact of a positive foreign demand shock on the euro area depends on the extent to which the shock translates into trade internal to the region or external. In this context, structural changes related to the globalisation of production processes, most notably the higher import content of exports, are found to play an important role in explaining the above puzzle, including reshaping the trade impacts of exchange rate movements.

Finally, chapter 6 (Gauging the labour market effects of international trade openness: an application to the US manufacturing sector, by Paul Hiebert and Isabel Vansteenkiste) seeks to quantify the extent to which the labour market has been affected by increasing trade openness. The chapter assesses the disproportionate weakness in US manufacturing employment following the 2002 recovery using input-output matrices and, alternatively, a sectoral vector auto-regressive (VAR) analysis. Based on the above two methodologies, some conclusions can be drawn regarding the impact of trade on employment and wages in the manufacturing sector. First, while a secular increase in the estimated net outflows of US manufacturing sector employment in response to trade has been apparent for the last two decades, such outflows appear to have intensified in recent years. At the same time, the employment response following an increase in trade openness remains muted. Second, a geographical breakdown reveals that China is becoming increasingly important; this seems to occur to a large extent at the expense of other Asian countries, however. Third, a sectoral breakdown reveals that the impact in the United States has been highest in low-skilled manufacturing sectors. Finally, real wages appear to respond negatively to increased trade openness.

Overall, the book underlines the relationships between globalisation and regionalism and assesses the extent to which increased global and regional integration has changed the functioning of the world economy. Globalisation and regionalism have fostered international trade and contributed to important changes in production processes, which have become internationalised to a great extent. As a result, the international transmission of shocks and the sensitivity of economies to their international environment have changed dramatically. At the same time, such changes have implied numerous adjustments in the functioning of the economies in reaction to the increasing importance of global and regional factors. Overall, the large efficiency gains associated with increased global and regional integration tend to more than compensate for the short-term costs resulting from such adjustments.

1   International linkages in the context of global and regional integration

Stephane Dees, Filippo di Mauro and Warwick J. McKibbin[1]

1   Introduction

Fewer barriers to international transactions and rapidly spreading information technology lie at the root of the accelerating integration of markets worldwide. Although not a new phenomenon, 'globalisation' has become a popular term since the 1990s to describe the increasingly integrated and interdependent world economy, which has led to higher trade, production and services outsourcing, as well as the migration of highly skilled professionals (Hummels, 2007). As these developments have unfolded, economic integration at a regional level has also strengthened, as a result of tighter institutional arrangements as well as substantial pressure from market forces.

Every single country in the world is now a member of regional trade agreements and at least one regional bloc. More than one-third of world trade takes place within such arrangements. All regional agreements have the objective of reducing barriers to trade between member countries and therefore, implicitly, of discriminating against trade with non-member countries. At their simplest level, RTAs aim at reducing or removing altogether tariffs on trade flows between member countries, with some also eliminating non-tariff barriers and liberalising investment flows. At their deepest level, RTAs have the objective of achieving economic union, implying the creation of common institutions (Schiff and Winters, 2003).

Are globalisation and regionalism part of the same phenomenon, which leads to closer economic relationships between countries? Does globalisation tend to increase regional integration, and how? How has increasing economic integration, both at the regional and the global level, affected the functioning of the global economy? What are the consequences of

[1] Respectively Principal Economist, European Central Bank; and Head of Division, European Central Bank; and Professor and Director, Centre for Applied Macroeconomic Analysis, ANU College of Business and Economics, Australian National University, Professional Fellow, the Lowy Institute for International Policy, and Non-resident Senior Fellow, the Brookings Institution.

globalisation and regionalism for world trade, for production processes and for domestic economies? What kind of economic adjustments do these phenomena imply in terms of factor mobility and relative costs? These are the overarching questions this book attempts to tackle.

This chapter gives a first overview of studies available on the two phenomena and tries to provide some initial answers to the above questions. It has the further aim of creating an overall perspective on the subject in order to situate the more specific aspects studied in subsequent chapters. Section 2 shows how globalisation and regional integration have been proceeding hand in hand in recent years. Section 3 examines how global factors impact on the functioning of domestic economies and how they interact with regional linkages. It also shows how increasing global and regional integration have changed the international transmission of shocks between countries. Finally, section 4 attempts to assess how greater global and regional integration has modified the international allocation of resources.

2   Relationship between globalisation and regionalism

2.1   The conceptual framework

In the last couple of decades regional trade – as measured by the trade among participants in a regional trade agreement – has grown more rapidly than global trade. Even in more mature trade groups, intra-regional trade has tended to increase since the 1970s. In America, in particular, the share of intra-regional trade has grown by some 50 per cent since the 1970s. In Europe the increase has been more modest, from 61 per cent to 67 per cent, reflecting the fact that the level of integration was already high (table 1.1). In Asia, the share of trade within regional groups (ASEAN, BA, GCC) has also grown but remains well below the share of trade taking place with the rest of the region.

The relationship between regionalism and globalisation tends to be depicted in the literature in two extreme ways: either as open regionalism aimed at integrating participating economies in the global market, or as a way to resist global market forces. In other words, regionalism emerges either as an outcome of, or as a response to, globalisation, depending on whether the relationship is accommodating or antagonistic (Nesadurai, 2002). The former – open regionalism – is, however, the dominant model in the literature.

There is no clear consensus regarding the impact of regional integration on globalisation. On the one hand, Bhagwati and Panagariya (1996) conclude that regionalism diverts trade by creating preferential treatment

Table 1.1 *Share of intra-regional/group trade as a percentage of total trade by region (1970–2004)*

Region	Trade group	Type of trade	Average 1970s	Average 1980s	Average 1990s	2000–4
Europe	EU 25	Within group	60.8	61.1	65.6	67.0
		With rest of region	10.4	9.6	6.9	6.7
	EU 15		*59.9*	*60.9*	*62.2*	*61.4*
	Eurozone		*51.9*	*50.4*	*51.7*	*50.5*
America	FTAA	Within group	46.2	46.6	53.0	60.3
		With rest of region	1.3	0.7	0.4	0.5
	Mercosur	Within group	9.0	7.7	18.5	14.5
		With rest of region	26.1	30.7	28.7	34.3
	NAFTA	Within group	36.8	39.4	47.0	55.9
		With rest of region	8.7	6.9	6.3	5.5
Africa	SADC	Within group	2.6	1.6	8.5	9.0
		With rest of region	0.6	0.5	1.9	3.1
	UEMOA	Within group	8.6	10.1	11.2	13.1
		With rest of region	6.0	6.9	13.5	15.9
Asia	ASEAN	Within group	18.2	18.4	22.1	22.4
		With rest of region	38.7	40.5	35.1	37.7
	BA	Within group	2.2	1.8	5.8	9.4
		With rest of region	36.5	46.1	46.8	41.0
	GCC	Within group	3.2	6.1	6.8	5.1
		With rest of region	33.2	46.2	54.4	59.1
Inter-regional	APEC	Within group	58.1	64.6	70.5	72.8

Note: FTAA = Free Trade Area of the Americas; Mercosur = Southern Common Market; NAFTA = North American Free Trade Agreement; SADC = Southern African Development Community; UEMOA = West African Economic and Monetary Union, ASEAN = Association of South-East Asian Nations; BA = Bangkok Agreement; GCC = Gulf Cooperation Council; and APEC = Asia-Pacific Economic Cooperation.

Source: United Nations Conference on Trade and Development (UNCTAD).

for the members of a RTA vis-à-vis non-members and argue that countries might lose interest in the multilateral system when they engage actively in regional initiatives. On the other hand, the proponents of regionalism (such as Bergsten, 1997) argue that RTAs enhance rather than reduce the prospects for global trade liberalisation as trade creation generally exceeds trade diversion. Such a stance promotes a view of regionalism as combining the benefits of regional integration without jeopardising the strengths of multilateralism.

One aspect that all agree on, however, is that globalisation and regionalism are not mutually exclusive and cannot be seen in isolation from each other. Indeed, globalisation may imply stronger links at the regional level. Moreover, trading blocs encourage trade within specific regions, possibly creating positive externalities in the rest of the world that might take the form of trade creation. Empirically, Lee and Shin (2006) find that, if an RTA involves geographically proximate countries (measured either by distance or by sharing a common border), trade increases significantly between them. At the same time, geographical proximity also contributes to increasing trade between members and non-members. In particular, they find that the east Asian RTAs are likely to create more trade between members without diverting trade from non-members.

2.2   *The role of vicinity*

As pointed out by Leamer (2006), 'trade in products is a neighbourhood experience', as trade flows decline dramatically with the distance despite the relative fall in transportation and communication costs. More than 20 per cent of world trade by value occurs between countries that share a land border. This level has remained nearly constant over recent decades, although it varies significantly between continents. For Africa, the Middle East and Asia between 1 and 5 per cent of trade by value is with neighbouring countries, but the figure is between 10 and 20 per cent for Latin American trade and between 25 and 35 per cent for European and North American trade (Hummels, 2007).

Gravity models have been widely used to describe bilateral trade in goods. Chapter 2, by Bussière and Schnatz, shows that the collapse of communism in central and eastern Europe, together with China's progress towards a more market-based economy since the early 1990s, have also been major factors fostering globalisation and triggering a significant reorientation of international trade flows. Bussière and Schnatz's use of a gravity model indicates that the industrialised countries still tend to display above-average trade integration (or trade openness) and that, among emerging market economies, it is mainly south-east Asian countries that show a high degree of integration. While China is also found to be rather well integrated into the world economy, many central and eastern European countries are far less integrated, the exceptions being the Czech Republic, Hungary and Poland. The CEEC results suggest that their trade integration with major euro area countries, particularly Germany, Italy and Austria, is already rather well advanced, however, in line with the regionalism forces at play within Europe. There is still significant scope for stronger trade links, nonetheless, particularly with more distant countries such as Japan and the United States, as well as emerging markets in Asia and Latin America.

2.3   The impact of production delocalisation

As pointed out by Ethier (2005), the main new feature of the present increase in globalisation is the associated changes in production processes, which have been internationalised to a great extent. While previous globalisation waves involved the exchange of goods, the current wave features what Grossman and Rossi-Hansberg (2006) call the 'trade in tasks' (also called 'outsourcing', 'offshoring' or 'production fragmentation').

The outsourcing of production has actually resulted in the rapid growth of trade in parts and components ('fragments' or 'middle products') at a rate exceeding that of the trade in final goods, due also to the more frequent multiple border crossings of unfinished products. Audet (1996), Campa and Goldberg (1997), Hummels, Rapoport and Yi (1998) and Yeats (2001) have used trade in intermediate inputs or in parts and components to measure outsourcing. Based on these various pieces of evidence, Grossman and Helpman (2005) conclude that the outsourcing of intermediate goods and business services is one of the most rapidly growing components of international trade.

In chapter 3, Athukorala and Yamashita show that the degree of dependence on the trade in parts and components is proportionately larger in east Asia than it is in North America and Europe. In particular, the rapid integration of China into the regional production networks and the related increase in production fragmentation in the region have boosted the dynamism of the east Asian economies. Kaminski and Ng (2005) also provide strong empirical support to the increasing integration of central European countries into global (and mostly EU-based) production and distribution networks.

Grossman and Rossi-Hansberg (2006) have identified a productivity effect that results from increased outsourcing (or 'task trade'). A decline in the cost of task trade acts like a boost to the productivity of the factor whose tasks become easier to outsource abroad. Chapter 4, by Geisheker, Görg and Taglioni, investigates productivity differences between multinationals, exporters and purely domestic firms using firm-level data from the whole euro area. They show that firms that establish affiliates abroad are larger, more profitable and more productive than firms that do not.

Moreover, there are performance premia (in terms of size, profits and productivity) for multinationals with a larger number of affiliates abroad.

3   Globalisation, regionalism and the international transmission of shocks

The forces of globalisation and regionalism are likely to change the way that disturbances are transmitted within an economy and throughout the various regions and the world economy. To quantify such impacts across major economic areas we present here a number of model results, referring first to global and then to regional factors.

3.1   The role of global factors in domestic economies

It is often argued that global and regional integration has led in recent decades to a greater degree of business cycle synchronisation between the main economies. Analysis of the contemporaneous correlations between domestic variables and the corresponding foreign variables may potentially shed light on the degree of synchronisation across economies. The foreign variables used in such an exercise are those included in the GVAR model,[2] a VAR-based model of the global economy. Table 1.2 shows the average correlation for selected countries between quarterly changes in gross domestic product (GDP), inflation and selected asset prices (equity prices, the exchange rate and interest rates) and those in the respective foreign variables over the period from the first quarter of 1979 to the fourth quarter of 2005. The correlation between domestic and foreign variables is fairly high for both output (between 0.4 and 0.5) and inflation (between 0.4 and 0.7). The correlation for output is lower for Japan, which is explained by some persistent weakness in the Japanese economy during this period. The correlations for output and inflation are also low for China, as the Chinese economy was much less open during the 1980s and the beginning of the 1990s. The fact that the euro area has the highest correlation for output growth confirms the evidence for a somewhat greater sensitivity to changes in conditions in the international environment of economic activity in the euro area relative to the other advanced

---

[2] The GVAR (global vector auto-regressive) model consists of a comprehensive framework that considers the responses to various types of global and country shocks through a number of transmission channels, including both trade flows and financial linkages. The GVAR model includes twenty-six economic areas, linked through area-specific vector error-correcting models allowing for simultaneous interrelations between domestic and foreign variables. For a more detailed description of the GVAR model, see Dees *et al.* (2007).

Table 1.2 *Correlation between quarterly changes in domestic and foreign variables (1984 Q1–2005 Q4) (correlation coefficients)*

	United States	Euro area	Japan	United Kingdom	China
Real output	0.46	0.52	0.16	0.36	0.07
Consumer price inflation	0.38	0.56	0.66	0.74	0.23
Real equity prices	0.79	0.83	0.54	0.78	–
Short-term interest rates	0.10	0.23	0.05	0.17	0.16
Long-term interest rates	0.81	0.73	0.49	0.57	–

Note: – = data not available.

Table 1.3 *Contemporaneous effects of foreign variables on their domestic counterparts (1979 Q1–2005 Q4)*

Country	Domestic variables[1]				
	y	D_p	q	r^S	r^L
United States	0.54	0.06	–	–	–
	[3.12][2]	[0.87]			
Euro area	0.53	0.25	1.15	0.09	0.63
	[4.03]	[3.31]	[8.90]	[3.84]	[7.86]
China	−0.1	0.61	–	0.12	–
	[−0.66]	[2.30]		[2.27]	
Japan	0.5	−0.04	0.67	−0.05	0.48
	[3.47]	[−0.38]	[5.53]	[−0.89]	[4.84]
United Kingdom	0.33	−0.15	0.84	0.27	0.67
	[2.33]	[−0.64]	[13.28]	[1.48]	[4.85]

Notes:
[1] y = real GDP, D_p = consumer price inflation, q = real equity prices, r^S = short-term interest rates and r^L = long-term interest rates.
[2] White's heteroskedastic robust t-ratios are given in square brackets.

economies. There is also evidence that this correlation has increased for the euro area in the last decade.

The direct effect of developments in the international economic environment on the various economies can be formally assessed from the estimated coefficients of the contemporaneous foreign variables in the GVAR equations for the corresponding domestic variables. These coefficients can be interpreted as impact elasticities between domestic and foreign variables. Table 1.3 presents the contemporaneous effects of foreign variables on their domestic counterparts. Most of these elasticities are significant and have a positive sign, as expected. They are particularly informative with regard to the international linkages between the domestic and foreign variables. Focusing on the euro area, we can see that a 1 per cent change in foreign real output in a given quarter leads to an increase of 0.5 per cent in euro area real output within the same quarter. Similar foreign output elasticities are obtained across the different regions, though the effect is slightly weaker for the United Kingdom. The absence of a significant output coefficient for China reflects the fact that the opening up of the economy is only recent. The relatively large and statistically significant elasticity estimate obtained in the case of the euro area is to a great extent a reflection of the high degree of trade openness of the euro area economy.

3.2   The role of regional factors

If increased integration into the global economy is likely to have made economies more sensitive to their international environment, regional integration might have dampened the sensitiveness of domestic economies to global developments. Dees and Vansteenkiste (2007) decompose economic shocks into three potential sources: unforeseen common shocks; unforeseen idiosyncratic (domestic or regional) shocks; and the spillover effects of unforeseen idiosyncratic shocks to other countries. While spillover effects appear to play only a secondary role, GDP developments are mostly explained by idiosyncratic and common shocks. In particular, emerging Asia tends to be most affected by regional shocks, while common shocks and spillover effects remain relatively limited. In contrast, the developed economies are less affected by regional shocks but appear more sensitive to common shocks.

Kose, Otrok and Whiteman (2003) find that a common world factor is an important driver of business cycles. They also find, however, that region-specific factors play only a minor role in explaining fluctuations in economic activity. Dees and Vansteenkiste (2007) also find that, for the euro area, common shocks appear more important than idiosyncratic shocks in the period 1979–92. Nonetheless, the most recent period shows an increase in the role of regional shocks as opposed to spillovers or common shocks. This is confirmed by other studies that show the existence of a European cycle (e.g. Christodoulakis et al., 1995, Artis and Zhang, 1997, Lumsdaine and Prasad, 2003, and Böwer and Guillemineau, 2006). A recent update of the work by Kose, Otrok and Whiteman (reported in International Monetary Fund [IMF], 2007) shows the increasing role of regional factors. It is still found that the global factor generally plays a more important role in explaining business cycles in industrial countries than in emerging market and developing countries. With more updated data, however, regional factors are now the most important in North America, Europe and Asia, where they explain more than 20 per cent of

Table 1.4 *Contributions to output fluctuations (unweighted averages for each region; percent)*

	Factors			
	Global	Regional	Country	Idiosyncratic
			1960–2005	
North America	16.9	51.7	14.8	16.6
Western Europe	22.7	21.6	34.6	21.1
Oceania	5.6	3.9	61.8	28.7
Emerging Asia and Japan	7.0	21.9	47.4	23.7
Latin America	9.1	16.6	48.6	25.7
Sub-Saharan Africa	5.3	2.7	40.7	51.3
Middle East and north Africa	6.3	6.3	53.8	33.6
			1960–85	
North America	31.4	36.4	15.7	16.5
Western Europe	26.6	20.5	31.6	21.3
Oceania	10.7	5.9	50.5	32.9
Emerging Asia and Japan	10.6	9.5	50.5	29.4
Latin America	16.2	19.4	41.2	23.2
Sub-Saharan Africa	7.2	5.1	39.7	48.0
Middle East and north Africa	8.9	5.1	49.1	36.9
			1986–2005	
North America	5.0	62.8	8.2	24.0
Western Europe	5.6	38.3	27.6	28.5
Oceania	9.4	25.9	31.1	33.6
Emerging Asia and Japan	6.5	34.7	31.1	27.7
Latin America	7.8	8.7	51.7	31.8
Sub-Saharan Africa	6.7	4.7	37.3	51.3
Middle East and north Africa	4.7	6.6	52.8	35.9

Note: The table shows the fraction of the variance of output growth attributable to each factor.

Source: IMF staff calculations.

the output fluctuations. This increasing role of regional factors is also confirmed in the IMF work by estimation over two sub-periods, 1960–85 and 1986–2005 (table 1.4). The results suggest that the global factor has, on average, played a less important role in the later period. At the same time, regional factors have become more important, especially in regions where trade and financial linkages have increased, as in North America, Europe and Asia. For Asia, these results are consistent with those found by Moneta and Rüffer (2006).

Beyond the role of regional factors in the business cycles, an important issue relates to the role of regional integration in the international transmission of shocks. In chapter 5, Anderton and di Mauro detail the transmission mechanisms from foreign factors to euro area domestic demand, and underline the degree in which interactions within the euro area may have dampened foreign demand shocks. They show that the ultimate impact of a positive foreign demand shock on the euro area depends on the extent to which the shock translates into internal or external trade. In this context, structural changes related to the globalisation of production processes, most notably the higher import penetration from low-cost countries as well as the higher import content of exports, are found to play an important role and may be causing changes in the impacts of foreign shocks.

Overall, while globalisation has caused economies to become more sensitive to global shocks, regional factors seem to have played an increasing role in recent decades, not only as an independent source of shocks but also as a force modifying the impact of common shocks on individual countries participating in regional groups.

4   Globalisation and regionalism: impact on factors and income

As globalisation and regionalism have made domestic economies more sensitive to global and regional developments, numerous adjustments have been needed in the functioning of these economies, especially in terms of the allocation of resources and income. In this section, we focus on the impact that globalisation and regionalism have on labour and capital allocation, including income distribution and economic welfare.

4.1   Impact on labour markets

Production delocalisation has allowed firms to adjust production processes in response to changes in the economic environment, bringing about deep changes in the international division of labour (Grossman and Rossi-Hansberg, 2006). At the same time, technological change has also led to dramatic changes in the reallocation of the production factors. Both globalisation and technological change therefore, have been implicated in a substantial reallocation of labour.

In chapter 6, Hiebert and Vansteenkiste seek to quantify the extent to which technological versus trade factors have an impact on the US labour market. They find that higher import competition appears to have manifested itself through real wage rather than employment adjustment in the US manufacturing sector.

Concerning the specific impact of production outsourcing on labour markets, the empirical literature concludes that the number of job losses brought about by delocalisation remains marginal. As reviewed by Mankiw and Swagel (2006), the empirical evidence suggests that increased employment in the overseas affiliates of US multinationals is associated with more employment in the US parent company rather than less.

The degree of labour mobility, including immigration policy or labour market legislation, is also key to explaining labour market adjustments. Although there is evidence that migration responds to regional economic disparities, the speed at which it does so is low and has been decreasing since the second half of the 1970s (Fatás, 2000). Moreover, the impact of labour migration on the employment of non-migrants has proved to remain very limited and short-lived.

4.2   Impact on capital flows

Global and regional forces have also played a major role in boosting global capital flows. While emerging markets should offer investment opportunities and therefore attract capital flows from advanced economies, emerging economies have actually registered financial account deficits (mainly China and the oil-exporting countries). At the same time, some advanced economies (mainly the United States) have registered large surpluses. This phenomenon can be explained, first, by the desire of Asian countries to build up large amounts of international reserves. Second, the sustained high growth rate of the Chinese economy has led to a sharp increase in trade in commodities, implying that commodity-exporting countries should benefit from higher revenues. Finally, the most advanced economies still represent attractive investment opportunities, absorbing as a result a large share of these excess savings.

Regional forces are also important in explaining capital flows, as shown by the results of gravity models, which are usually used for explaining trade flows. Looking at cross-border equity flows, Portes and Rey (2005) find that distance, which proxies information asymmetries, is a surprisingly large barrier to cross-border asset trade. The establishment of the EMU, for instance, enhanced regional financial integration in the euro area in both equity and bond markets. After controlling for the effect of a set of variables borrowed from the literature on finance, De Santis and Gérard (2006) show that euro area investors assign a higher weight to portfolio investment in euro area countries.

Finally, Aviat and Coeurdacier (2007) find evidence of a complementarity between bilateral trade in goods and bilateral asset holdings. Using a simultaneous gravity equations framework, they show that a 10 per cent increase in bilateral trade raises bilateral asset holdings by 6 to 7 per cent. The reverse causality is also significant, albeit smaller. Controlling for trade, however, the impact of distance on asset holdings is drastically reduced.

4.3   Impact on wages

Trade integration and production outsourcing are often quoted as promoting a rise in inequality, especially through their impact on wages. The outsourcing of less skilled jobs to other countries has indeed increased the demand for high-skilled workers in developed economies, leading to a relative fall in the wages of the less skilled workers. Globalisation is not the only factor affecting wage distribution, however. Technological progress, by raising the productivity of high-skilled workers, is another factor that is often mentioned. Just as with the effects on employment, it is difficult to distinguish the impact on relative wages due to outsourcing from that arising from skill-biased technological change. Feenstra and Hanson (1996) show that both outsourcing and high-tech equipment are important explanations for the increase in the relative share of skilled labour in the United States, though it needs to be emphasised that the relative contributions of the two sources are highly sensitive to how 'high-tech equipment' is defined.

Moreover, regardless of how outsourcing affects the relative wages, outsourcing leads to an increase in firms' productivity, lowering the prices for final goods. If such a fall is larger than the one in nominal wages, the real wages of all workers might improve. Grossman and Rossi-Hansberg (2006) show that the real wage of less skilled workers is 'guaranteed' to rise as a result of the productivity-enhancing effect of outsourcing.

Concerning the impact of migration on wages, Feenstra (2007) nuances the negative effects usually advanced for the US economy. There are found to be two offsetting factors. First, there can be an increase in industries employing the immigrants, leading these workers to be absorbed without a decrease in wages. Second, immigrants coming to the United States are at different education levels – either less or more educated – from the majority of the US population, allowing for some complementary effects of immigrants on local wages. As a consequence, and allowing for adjustments in output and capital stocks by industries, Feenstra shows that immigration has a complementary effect on wages for many workers.

4.4   Impact on prices

When assessing the welfare gains of increasing trade integration, one needs to account for the impact on consumer prices. Increasing trade openness may have influenced the behaviour of inflation through various channels, both direct and indirect. The main direct effect is through increased competition in internationally traded goods from low-cost suppliers in emerging economies. This has resulted in rising imports and increased competition in domestic markets, ultimately leading to a fall in both real import prices and in the prices of domestic goods exposed to international competition. For instance, Kamin, Marazzi and Schindler (2006) estimate the direct impact of increased Chinese imports on annual consumer price inflation globally at −0.1 percentage points (pp). For the euro area, ECB estimates (ECB, 2006) indicate that the increase in import penetration from low-cost countries may have dampened euro area import price inflation by 2.1 pp on average each year, an effect almost equally accounted for by China and the European Union's new member states (NMS). Such an impact is decomposed into two components, the first due to changes in the import share (the 'share effect'), capturing the impact of the lower price level of low-cost import suppliers (1.6 pp per annum), and the second due to changes in import prices (the 'price effect'), capturing the impact of lower import price inflation from the low-cost countries relative to the high-cost ones (0.5 pp per annum).

More indirectly, increased international competition may have limited the pricing power of domestic corporations. At the same time, it may have enhanced the incentives for firms to innovate. The effect of globalisation on productivity may be partly related to a better diffusion of ideas or technological progress, reflecting the importance of foreign direct investment (FDI) and the integration of production processes. In addition, fiercer competition from low-cost suppliers may have driven the least efficient domestic producers out of the market.

All in all, therefore, while globalisation forces may have caused higher commodity prices, through higher demand for new materials and energy, they have also exerted substantial downward pressure on consumer prices as low-cost imports have increased sharply. The latter appears to have had a greater impact than the former on final prices.

5   Conclusions

This chapter has looked at the relationships between globalisation and regionalism and assessed the extent to which increased global and regional integration have changed economic relationships at the level of firms, countries, regions and the world.

Globalisation and regionalism are not mutually exclusive and cannot be seen in isolation from each other. In particular, it is seen that trading blocs, when envisaged as 'open regionalism', not only encourage trade within specific regions but also create positive externalities for the rest of the world. Regionalism is also justified by the fact that, despite the reduction in transportation and communication costs, vicinity between countries still represents the main determinant of trade flows. The entry of new players in the global economic structure (notably the central and eastern European countries and China) has strengthened regional integration forces even further, especially in Europe and Asia.

At the same time, global and regional integration has also been characterised by important changes in production processes, which have become internationalised to a great extent. The outsourcing of production, through regional production networks, has actually fostered the development of international production fragmentation within regions. By increasing productivity, increased outsourcing has not only reinforced trade activity but has also impacted positively on the performance of firms, which are shown to be more profitable and more productive when they establish affiliates abroad.

By modifying trade patterns and production processes, the trends towards globalisation and regionalism have altered the way that disturbances are transmitted within an economy and throughout the regions and the world economy. While increased integration into the global economy has made economies more sensitive to their international environment, regional integration has also dampened somewhat the sensitivity of domestic economies to global developments. At the same time, such changes have implied numerous adjustments in the functioning of economies in response to the increasing importance of global and regional factors. It is important, however, to distinguish between adjustments that are directly attributable to globalisation and regionalism and those that are linked to other factors. For instance, opponents of globalisation often associate decreasing manufacturing employment and raising inequalities in industrialised economies with increases in delocalisation. It is shown, however, that technological changes occurring at the same time might have generated a larger impact on labour markets and income distribution, while the effects of global and regional integration remain, overall, relatively limited. Moreover, globalisation and regionalism have tended to increase the purchasing power of consumers in industrialised countries, as the forces of globalisation have exerted substantial downward pressure on consumer prices through the sharp increase in low-cost imports.

In summary, globalisation and regionalism have been responsible for significant changes in the global economy. By increasing trade flows and fostering the internationalisation of production processes, economies have become more sensitive to global and regional factors. By going global, firms have had the opportunity to outsource some parts of their production processes, increasing their efficiency and therefore their performance, but implying also in the short term some adjustment in their factor allocation. In particular, the delocalisation of tasks from industrialised countries to low-cost countries has led to concerns in terms of labour market developments (especially in labour-intensive and low-skilled sectors in the industrialised economies). Overall, however, it is largely recognised that such short-term costs have remained limited and that globalisation and regionalism have mostly positive effects at the domestic and global levels.

References

Audet, D. (1996), 'Globalization in the Clothing Industry', in *Globalization of Industry: Overview and Sector Reports* (Paris: Organisation for Economic Co-operation and Development), 323–55.

Artis, M. J., and W. Zhang (1997), 'International Business Cycles and the ERM: Is There a European Business Cycle?', *International Journal of Finance and Economics*, **2**, 1, 1–16.

Aviat, A., and N. Coeurdacier (2007), 'The Geography of Trade in Goods and Asset Holdings', *Journal of International Economics*, **71**, 1, 22–51.

Bergsten, C. F. (1997), 'Open Regionalism', Working Paper no. 97-3, Peterson Institute for International Economics, Washington, DC.

Bhagwati, A., and A. Panagariya (1996), 'Preferential Trade Areas and Multilateralism: Strangers, Friends, or Foes?', in A. Bhagwati and A. Panagariya (eds.), *The Economics of Preferential Trade Agreements* (Washington, DC: American Enterprise Institute and AEI Press), 1–78.

Böwer, U., and C. Guillemineau (2006), 'Determinants of Business Cycle Synchronisation across Euro Area Countries', Working Paper no. 587, European Central Bank, Frankfurt.

Campa, J. M., and L. S. Goldberg (1997), 'The Evolving External Orientation of Manufacturing Industries: Evidence from Four Countries', *Federal Reserve Bank of New York Economic Policy Review*, **3**, 2, 53–81.

Christodoulakis, N., S. P. Dimelis and T. Kollintzas (1995), 'Comparisons of Business Cycles in the EC: Idiosyncracies and Regularities', *Economica*, **62**, 1–27.

De Santis, R. A., and B. Gérard (2006), 'Financial Integration, International Portfolio Choice and the European Monetary Union', Working Paper no. 626, European Central Bank, Frankfurt.

Dees, S., F. di Mauro, M. H. Pesaran and L. V. Smith (2007), 'Exploring the International Linkages of the Euro Area: A Global VAR Analysis', *Journal of Applied Econometrics*, **22**, 1, 1–38.

Dees, S., and I. Vansteenkiste (2007), 'The Transmission of US Cyclical Developments to the Rest of the World', Working Paper no. 798, European Central Bank, Frankfurt.

ECB (2006), 'Effects of the rising trade integration of low-cost countries on euro area import prices', *Monthly Bulletin*, August, 56–7.

Ethier, W. J. (2005), 'Globalization, Globalisation: Trade, Technology, and Wages', *International Review of Economics and Finance*, **14**, 3, 237–58.

Fatás, A. (2000), 'Intranational Labor Migration, Business Cycles, and Growth', in G. D. Hess and E. van Wincoop (eds.), *Intranational Macroeconomics* (Cambridge: Cambridge University Press), 156–88.

Feenstra, R. C. (2007), 'Globalization and Its Impact on Labor', Global Economy Lecture, Vienna Institute for International Economic Studies, 8 February.

Feenstra, R. C., and G. H. Hanson (1996), 'Foreign Investment, Outsourcing and Relative Wages', in R. C. Feenstra, G. M. Grossman and D. A. Irwin (eds.), *The Political Economy of Trade Policy: Papers in Honor of Jagdish Bhagwati* (Cambridge, MA: MIT Press), 89–129.

Grossman, G. M., and E. Helpman (2005), 'Outsourcing in a global economy', *Review of Economic Studies*, 72, 1, 135–59.

Grossman, G. M., and E. Rossi-Hansberg (2006), 'Trading Tasks: a Simple Model of Outsourcing', Working Paper no. 12721, National Bureau of Economic Research, Cambridge, MA.

Hummels, D. (2007), 'Transportation Costs and International Trade in the Second Era of Globalization', *Journal of Economic Perspectives*, 21, 3, 131–54.

Hummels, D., D. Rapoport and K.-M. Yi (1998), 'Vertical specialization and the changing nature of world trade', *Federal Reserve Bank of New York Economic Policy Review*, 4, 2, 79–99.

IMF (2007), *World Economic Outlook* (Washington, DC: International Monetary Fund).

Kamin, S. B., M. Marazzi and J. W. Schindler (2006), 'The Impact of Chinese Exports on Global Import Prices', *Review of International Economics*, 14, 2, 179–201.

Kaminski, B., and F. Ng (2005), 'Production Disintegration and Integration of Central Europe into Global Markets', *International Review of Economics and Finance*, 14, 3, 377–90.

Kose, A. M., C. Otrok and C. H. Whiteman (2003), 'International Business Cycles: World, Religion, and Country-specific Factors', *American Economic Review*, 93, 4, 1216–39.

Leamer, E. E. (2006), 'A Flat World, a Level Playing Field, a Small World after all, or None of the Above? Review of Thomas L. Friedman, *The World is Flat*', *Journal of Economic Literature*, 45, 1, 83–126.

Lee, J.-W., and K. Shin (2006), 'Does Regionalism Lead to more Global Trade Integration in East Asia?', *North American Journal of Economics and Finance*, 17, 3, 283–301.

Lumsdaine, R. L., and E. S. Prasad (2003), 'Identifying the Common Component in International Economic Fluctuations: A New Approach', *Economic Journal*, 113, January, 101–27.

Mankiw, N. G., and P. Swagel (2006), 'The Politics and Economics of Offshore Outsourcing', *Journal of Monetary Economics*, 53, 5, 1027–56.

Moneta, F., and R. Rüffer (2006), 'Business Cycle Synchronisation in East Asia', Working Paper no. 671, European Central Bank, Frankfurt.

Nesadurai, H. (2002), 'Globalisation and Economic Regionalism: A Survey and Critique of the Literature', Working Paper no. 108/02, Centre for the Study of Globalisation and Regionalisation, University of Warwick, Warwick.

Portes, R., and H. Rey (2005), 'The Determinants of Cross-border Equity Flows', *Journal of International Economics*, **65**, 2, 269–96.

Schiff, M., and L. A. Winters (2003), *Regional Integration and Development* (Washington, DC: World Bank).

Yeats, A. J. (2001), 'Just How Big Is Global Production Sharing?', in S. W. Arndt and H. Kierzkowski (eds.), *Fragmentation: New Production Patterns in the World Economy* (Oxford: Oxford University Press), 108–43.

2   Trade integration of the central and eastern European countries and China: has it reached potential?

Matthieu Bussière and Bernd Schnatz[1]

1   Introduction

The emergence of China as a global player and the awakening of the central and eastern European countries after the fall of the 'Iron Curtain' have been breathtaking events, both for the euro area and for the global economy at large. This is strikingly evidenced by the reorientation of global flows in goods and service and the unprecedented speed at which trade integration of both China and the CEEC with western European economies has progressed since the beginning of the transition process in the early 1990s.[2] Not only did the brisk pace of market integration affect regional and global trade patterns, it also triggered tensions in the political and economic sphere, as it was perceived to affect adversely the competitiveness and employment situation in partner countries.

This chapter contributes to this policy debate by proposing a new benchmark measure for the trade intensity of the CEEC and China.[3] Overall, the dynamic growth of external trade with these transition economies is hardly surprising. The former inward orientation of these countries associated with central planning, their policy-induced geographical trade specialisation (e.g. within Comecon, the Council for Mutual Economic Assistance, for the CEEC), had to adjust towards more market-based structures as they opened up. The transformation of regional and global trading patterns was further fostered by the robust economic growth recorded in the transition countries over the past decade

---

[1] Respectively Economist and Principal Economist, European Central Bank.

[2] See also Bussière *et al.* (2005) and Bussière and Schnatz (2006).

[3] In this chapter, the 'CEEC' are defined as the eight new EU member states from this region, namely the Czech Republic, Estonia, Hungary, Latvia, Lithuania, Poland, the Slovak Republic and Slovenia. The 'NMS' refer to the CEEC plus Malta and Cyprus. The 'south-eastern European countries' include Albania, Bosnia, Bulgaria, Croatia, Macedonia, Moldova and Romania. The other Asian countries ('rest of Asia') encompass Hong Kong, Indonesia, Malaysia, the Philippines, Singapore, South Korea and Thailand.

or so, and – in the case of the CEEC – their geographical proximity to the euro area.

Against the background of the significant progress made over the past decade, the question arises as to how well these countries are integrated both into their respective regions and into the global economy. Answering such questions requires having a view on what would constitute a 'normal' degree of trade linkages of these countries. Standard measures of economic openness and trade shares provide only a limited guide to address these questions, as they are difficult to compare to more normative benchmarks. We use instead a gravity model, which controls for the size of the countries, their location and other fundamentals, to shed light on the overall degree of trade intensity of a large number of countries as well as the depth of their bilateral trade linkages with major economies. In spite of its simplicity, this model constitutes a convenient and tractable tool with relatively high explanatory power. This approach helps to identify whether, for instance, small open economies, which are commonly found to have a high trade to GDP ratio, are indeed well integrated into the world economy. It also confirms that regional free trade arrangements are associated with tighter trade linkages. Finally, we provide a data-based measure of globalisation trends in the world economy, suggesting that these factors raised trade on average by more than 2.5 per cent per year.

Overall, the results regarding the intensity of global and regional trade linkages suggest the following. (1) At a global level, the industrialised countries still tend to display above-average external trade intensity. (2) Among emerging market economies, it is mainly the south-east Asian countries that show high global trade intensity. (3) China is also found to be rather well integrated into the world economy; it has particularly strong trade links with natural-resource-rich countries – such as Canada and Australia – as well as with some regional trading partners in south-east Asia. (4) Many of the CEEC are far less integrated into the world economy, with the exceptions of the Czech Republic, Hungary and Poland; at a regional level, however, their external trade is relatively intense with several euro area countries and particularly strong within the central and eastern European region and with countries of the former Comecon.

The chapter is structured as follows. The next section presents some stylised facts about the external trade of these dynamic countries and regions with a special focus on the euro area. Subsequently, we present a gravity equation and derive a measure of overall trade intensity for individual countries and compare it to their trade integration with the CEEC and China. The last section concludes.

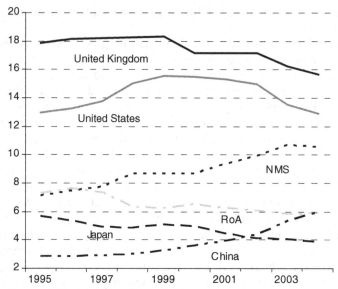

Source: ECB and ECB staff calculations.
Notes: Last observation refers to 2004. RoA refers to the 'Rest of Asia'.

Figure 2.1 Extra-euro area trade shares (percent of total extra-euro area trade, annual)

2   Changing euro area trade patterns: stylised facts

From a euro area perspective, the most striking patterns in extra-euro area trade since the 1990s have been the increases in the market share of the emerging markets, specifically the central and eastern European countries (particularly the new EU member states) and China.[4] By contrast, the share of the industrialised countries (Japan, the United Kingdom and, more recently, the United States) has tended to decrease (see figure 2.1).[5]

---

[4] In this chapter, the term 'new EU member states' refers to the ten countries that acceded to the European Union in 2004. It does not take into account the EU accession of Bulgaria and Romania in 2007 and treats Slovenia as an NMS, even though the country adopted the euro in 2007 and, thus, became a member of the euro area.

[5] Market shares refer to the percentage of import and export trade with a particular country relative to total trade. Extra-euro area trade excludes trade between the countries that are part of the euro area. In anticipation of using a gravity model, we follow standard practice and refer to overall trade. A separate assessment of exports and imports would require accounting for additional factors (such as competitiveness) to explain the difference between exports and imports. We leave this for future research.

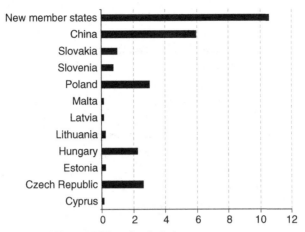

Source: ECB and ECB staff calculations.
Note: Last observation refers to 2004.

Figure 2.2 Trade shares of NMS and China in extra-euro area trade (2004) (percent of total extra-euro area trade)

Between 1995 and 2004 the share in extra-euro area trade of the NMS as a group – while being individually relatively small trading partners – has increased from 7.1 per cent to about 10.6 per cent. In 2004 it was exceeded only by the market shares of the United Kingdom (15.6 per cent) and the United States (12.9 per cent). Among the NMS, the market shares of Poland, the Czech Republic and Hungary are around 2 to 3 per cent, while the other countries' market shares are below 1 per cent (see figure 2.2). The market shares of the Baltic countries and of Cyprus and Malta are, not surprisingly, very small. For most of the NMS, growth in market shares was buoyant. Trade shares generally rose by more than 50 per cent over the ten-year reference period (see figure 2.3). Cyprus and Malta are exceptions. These two countries even recorded a small decline in their market share vis-à–vis the euro area, which may be related to the fact that they were not subject to the transitional changes observed in the other countries and their structural changes in their economies. In addition, Slovenia did not record a rise in market share over this period, which may be due to some trade diversion given the re-establishment of more stable market conditions in the Balkan countries during these ten years.

Looking at individual euro area countries, the trade of the CEEC rose particularly strongly with Germany, where the share of these countries is

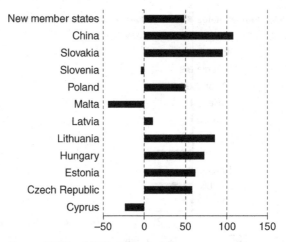

Source: ECB and ECB staff calculations.
Note: Last observation refers to 2004.

Figure 2.3 Growth in trade shares of NMS and China in extra-euro area trade (1995–2004) (percent of total extra-euro area trade, annual)

now higher than that of the United Kingdom and the United States and close to the share of France. For other large euro area countries, trade with the CEEC is less significant.

Another example of unprecedented integration dynamics is China, whose rise in market share has accelerated since 1999 (see figure 2.1). Overall, China has become the third largest trading partner in the world, behind the euro area and the United States. China's openness ratio – measured as the sum of exports and imports to GDP – almost doubled, from around 33 per cent to around 60 per cent, between 1995 and 2004. Consequently, the market share of China in extra-euro area trade also more than doubled over this period. Despite this, in 2004 its market share was still just above a half of the trade share of the NMS. Taking all the Asian countries (Japan, China and the 'rest of Asia' category) together, however, this region now constitutes the most important trading partner of the euro area.

The dynamic trade reorientation and integration of these countries both at the regional and at the global level raises the question of the 'natural' place of the CEEC and China in international markets in general, and in trade with the euro area in particular. This calls for a quantification of the role of these regions in international trade, given their economic size and location.

3   Evidence from a gravity model

3.1   *Suitability of the gravity model*

The preceding presentation of stylised facts suggests that the magnitudes and patterns of international trade are mainly affected by two factors: (1) the economic size of the countries that engage in trade and (2) the distance between them. The relevance of economic size is apparent from the fact that the larger CEEC in terms of GDP (Poland, Hungary and the Czech Republic) are more important for euro area trade than the smaller countries. At the same time, distance may explain why euro area trade with China is smaller than with the CEEC in spite of the larger economic weight of the former. Mainly reflecting their economic proximity, the other Asian emerging economies constitute the most important trading partners of China, once they are aggregated. Among these countries, Hong Kong and South Korea are the most important trading partners, followed by Singapore and Malaysia. Both distance and economic size could also explain why Germany has a much larger trade share with the CEEC than France and Italy, for instance.

Accordingly, the so-called gravity models appear to be well suited to determining a benchmark for a 'normal' degree of trade intensity between countries. From a theoretical point of view, these models are fully in line with standard international trade models (see Anderson and van Wincoop, 2003, and Deardorff, 1995). Following a specification reminiscent of Isaac Newton's gravitation theory, this class of models relates bilateral trade between two countries to their (economic) mass – commonly measured in terms of real GDP – and the geographical distance separating them. Four other factors affecting trade costs were identified. (1) Language: countries sharing the same language have lower transaction costs and tend historically to have more established trade ties (e.g. owing to a legacy of colonial ties). (2) Border: the transaction costs argument may also be relevant for neighbouring countries as the number of border crossings is smaller, which in times past may have been an important factor determining the exchange of goods. (3) Territory: countries that shared a common territory in the past (such as those of former Yugoslavia and the former Soviet Union) might have maintained closer trade ties than otherwise. (4) FTAs: membership of and participation in a free trade agreement (such as the European Union, NAFTA, ASEAN, etc.) may stimulate trade among the constituent countries.[6]

In more formal terms, the following gravity equation was estimated, in which all the variables included are defined in logarithms:

$$T_{ijt} = \alpha_{ij} + \theta_t + \beta_1 y_{ijt} + \beta_2 d_{ij} + \beta_3 q_{it} + \beta_4 q_{jt} + \sum_{k=1}^{K} \gamma_k Z_{ijkt} + \varepsilon_{ijt}$$

T_{ijt} is the magnitude of bilateral trade between country i and country j at time t (in real US dollar terms); y_{ijt} corresponds to the sum of y_{it} and y_{jt}, which stand for the (real) GDP in country i and country j, respectively, at time t; d_{ij} is the distance variable; and Z_k is a dummy variable for country pairs sharing a common language or a common border, having a common history or being members of the same free trade areas, as outlined above. The latter variable also accounts for regional integration effects. Real GDP per capita, which is often introduced in gravity models to control for the stage of economic development, was not included owing to collinearity problems between the fixed effects and population (see also Micco *et al.*, 2003). In line with the above discussion, we expect β_1 to have a positive sign, β_2 to show a negative sign and all γ_k to have a positive impact on the magnitude of bilateral trade. Following standard practice in the literature, trade is defined as the average of exports and imports, and distance is measured in terms of great circle distances between the capitals of country i and country j. As all trade figures are expressed in dollar terms, the real exchange rate, q, of each country against the dollar was included to control for valuation effects. Moreover, we included for trade involving Germany a dummy variable for German unification, which is zero before 1992 and one thereafter.

Of special relevance are the deterministic terms, as they are used in the following to construct indicators of bilateral trade intensity and globalisation effect. First, α_{ij} are the individual country-pair dummies (fixed effects) covering all unobservable factors affecting bilateral trade, as ignoring country heterogeneity can lead to highly distorted estimates (see Egger and Pfaffermayr, 2003). Indeed, a pooled estimation of the same model would give rather different coefficient estimates, underlining the importance of employing an appropriate estimation approach in order to achieve unbiased estimates. Furthermore, Micco *et al.* (2003) suggest that the inclusion of country-pair-specific effects may mitigate endogeneity

---

[6] We also considered adding FDI flows as an additional trade determinant, but there are several caveats: (1) the data are very volatile, (2) endogeneity problems could distort the estimates and (3) inspection of the data points to significant quality constraints.

problems. For instance, unusually high trade flows may lead to the establishment of a free trade agreement rather than vice versa. Fixed effects (FE) take into account whether two countries have traditionally traded a lot. Second, θ_t are the time-specific effects accounting for any variables affecting bilateral trade that vary over time and are constant across country pairs, such as global changes in transport and communication costs. They also control for common shocks or the general trend towards 'globalisation'. ε_{ij} is the error term.

The standard FE estimator precludes estimating the coefficients for d_{ij} and Z_k (apart from the dummies for the free trade areas). In order to account for this, an additional regression of the estimated country-pair effects on the time-invariant variables is run, for two reasons: first, this allows us to understand the importance of these variables for international trade; and, second, it purges the estimated fixed effects from the effects of the time-invariant variables (see Cheng and Wall, 2005).

$$\hat{\alpha}_{ij} = \beta_1 + \beta_2 d_{ij} + \sum_{k=1}^{K} \gamma_k Z_k + \mu_{ij}$$

Note that the error term of this last equation has an expected value of zero for the entire sample. For individual countries, however, it can be positive or negative, on average. Importantly, therefore, it can be interpreted as a measure of trade intensity, 'net of' the impact of the other explanatory variables. As a result, it represents a more meaningful alternative and more refined measure of trade 'openness' than the usual ratios of exports and imports to GDP or a country's world market share, as it takes into account the geographical location and the size of the country together with various idiosyncratic characteristics.

3.2 Data

The data set includes bilateral trade flows across sixty-one countries (for details, see the data appendix). These include most large trading nations but exclude countries relying strongly on oil exports, such as Saudi Arabia, as these countries' trade flows are likely to be determined by factors other than those applying to the rest of the countries in the sample, owing to the different trade structures. Accordingly, we also excluded the least developed countries, which often rely on just a few commodities. As usual in gravity models, we refer to overall trade, as a separate assessment of exports and imports would require accounting for additional factors (such as price and non-price competitiveness) to explain the discrepancy between exports and imports. The data are annual and span the period from 1980 to 2003. This amounts to more than 3,500 bilateral trade relationships and almost 53,000 observations in the standard fixed-effects regression.

The distance variable – measured as the aerial distance between the capitals of the two countries under consideration – is slightly modified, as it has some caveats. One drawback of this measure is that it implicitly assumes that overland transport costs are comparable to overseas transport costs. Moreover, it assumes that the capital city is the only economic centre of a country, which is probably more appropriate for small than for large countries. As the latter assumption appears to be particularly unsuited for China and the United States, the variable was adjusted for those two countries by using a weighted average of the distance of each country in the sample to five big cities in China and the four big cities in the United States.[7]

The dummy variable for common language was set equal to one if in both countries a significant part of the population speaks the same language (English, French, Spanish, Portuguese, German, Swedish, Dutch, Chinese, Malay, Russian, Greek, Arabic, Serbo-Croatian or Albanian). Some countries even enter more than one language grouping, such as Canada, where both English and French are native idioms, or Singapore, where English, Chinese and Malay are commonly understood languages. This, of course, implies the definition of a cut-off point; overall, there are 274 country pairs in which the same language is spoken (see data appendix for further details). The dummy variable for having a common border refers to 179 land borders shared by the countries included in the sample. Finally, dummy variables have been included for the most important free trade agreements, namely the European Union, ASEAN, NAFTA, CEFTA and Mercosur. The FTAs have been introduced or have expanded during the period of the analysis; hence, they were already included in this step.

3.3   Estimation results

In table 2.1, the first column shows our central estimation results following the two-step FE formulation proposed by Cheng and Wall (2005). The included variables generally have the expected sign and are statistically significant. The goodness of fit of the model is highly satisfactory, as the right-hand-side variables seem to explain a large fraction of the variance of the external trade. This implies that even such a fairly simple specification

---

[7] For the United States, New York (0.48), Los Angeles (0.23), Chicago (0.17) and Houston (0.12) were considered. For China, Shanghai (0.35), Beijing (0.20), Guangzhou (0.19), Chongquing (0.13) and Tianjin (0.13) were included. The numbers in parentheses are the respective weights.

Table 2.1 *Estimation results*

	FE	FE
	(1)	(2)
First-step regression		
GDP	0.57[a]	0.57[a]
EU	−0.00	–
Mercosur	0.23[b]	0.23[b]
NAFTA	0.45[a]	0.45[a]
CEFTA	0.22[a]	0.22[b]
Second-step regression		
Distance	−0.58[a]	−0.59[a]
Border	1.09[a]	1.13[a]
Language	1.22[a]	1.27[a]
Territory	0.33	–
EU	1.34[a]	1.31[a]
ASEAN	2.02[a]	1.98[a]
Mercosur	0.18	–
NAFTA	1.54[a]	1.48[a]
CEFTA	0.32	–
First stage		
R^2	0.64	0.64
Number of observations	52,724	52,724
Second stage		
R^2	0.37	0.37
Number of observations	3,413	3,413

Notes:
[a] = significant at the 1 per cent level; [b] = significant at the 5 per cent level.

of international trade is able to explain a significant part of the variation in international trade. The model confirms that economic size has a highly significant, albeit less than proportional, impact on bilateral trade. The coefficient of around 0.5 implies that a 1 per cent increase in GDP in each country is associated with a rise in world trade by about 1 per cent.

The dummies for FTAs enter significantly and with the right sign, with the exception of the EU dummy. The inclusion of the dummies for FTAs in the second step of the regression does yield a significant coefficient for the EU dummy, however. This reflects the fact that most member countries of the European Union joined a common free trade agreement long before the first observation in the sample, implying that – consistent with the proposition of FTAs' endogeneity (see Micco *et al.*, 2003) – the fixed effects already account for the effect of EU participation. At the same time, the dummies for Mercosur and CEFTA were insignificant in this second stage, suggesting that the establishment of these FTAs might not reflect strong initial trade relationships, while there might have been an effect from the creation of NAFTA. As expected, the distance term is negative and highly significant, implying that trade between any two countries is positively affected by geographical proximity. Similarly, having a common border and speaking the same language implies three times higher trade between the two countries than otherwise, while the common territory dummy is insignificant. Dropping insignificant variables from the specification barely changes the results (see table 2.1, second column).

The model estimates also successfully pass several robustness tests (see Bussière and Schnatz, 2006, for the detailed results). First, the results are compared to those deriving from a dynamic ordinary least squares (OLS) specification proposed by Kao and Chiang (2000) and implemented in a gravity model by Faruqee (2004). Employing such an estimator to account for possible non-stationarity in and cointegration among the variables (which also takes into account better the potential endogeneity autocorrelation issues by adding leads and lags for the differenced explanatory variables) gives estimates that are very close to the results of the FE estimator. This suggests that the potential bias from the FE specification should be small.

As a second robustness check, two alternative samples have been estimated. The first excludes the transition countries, as the inclusion of these countries may have undesirable effects on the estimates (see Bussière *et al.*, 2005). With the exception of the border and the language dummies – both of which fall noticeably – the results are very stable. The distance term is only slightly higher while the dummies included for FTAs are relatively close to the estimates shown before. For this sample, we also contrasted the results with the instrumental variables estimation technique proposed by Hausman and Taylor (1981), which permits the consistent estimation of the coefficients of the time-invariant variable. This technique also yields similar results. Once more the specification is very robust to using different econometric methods.

We also estimated the same specification again for the Organisation for Economic Co-operation and Development (OECD) countries only.[8] Although the number of observations drops by roughly 80 per cent, it is noteworthy that the coefficients retain their signs and significance. The coefficients remain close to those estimated in the full model. The dummy variable for NAFTA remains positive and significant but is smaller than in the previous specification; the EU dummy becomes significant and positive. The coefficients of the time-invariant variables are somewhat smaller. The fact that the goodness of fit of this regression is even better

---

[8] In this specification, several variables used in the full model drop out, as there are no relevant observations (e.g. Mercosur, CEFTA and common territory).

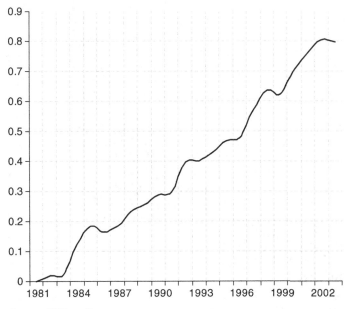

Source: ECB staff.
Note: The estimated time effects have been normalised to zero in 1981.

Figure 2.4 Globalisation index based on normalised time effects

than for the regression encompassing all countries suggests that the larger database possibly also exhibits more noise, as it includes many developing countries, making the sample more heterogeneous.

Finally, the time effects of the regression provide a gauge of the extent to which trade had increased for all countries from the early 1980s, irrespective of the growth in global economic activity and other gravity fundamentals (see figure 2.4). Accordingly, it provides a broad measure for globalisation in international trade. The estimated time effects (normalised to 1981) increased significantly over time. In 2003 they stood at almost 0.80, which suggests that international trade grew by 80 per cent over this period, or on average by more than 2.5 per cent per year, owing to globalisation effects alone.

3.4   Overall trade intensity indicators

Putting these elements into a gravity framework allows the derivation of an indicator of individual countries' average, or global, degree of 'trade

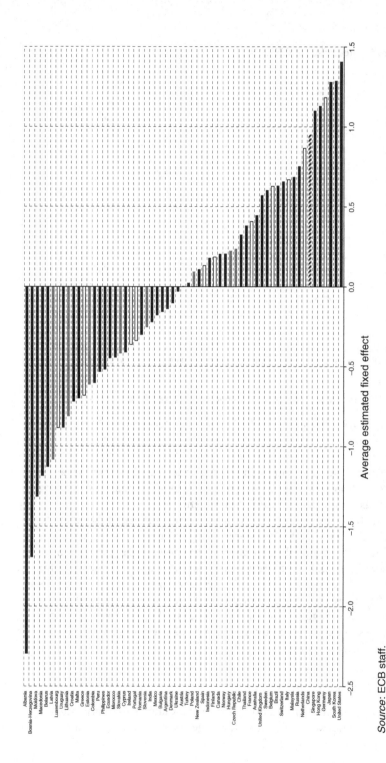

Average estimated fixed effect

Source: ECB staff.

Notes: The exponential of each indicator minus one can be interpreted as the multiple of the average degree of integration of each country. White bars indicate euro area countries, the dashed bar indicates China and grey bars indicate the CEEC. Black bars indicate all other countries in the sample.

Figure 2.5 Overall trade integration indicators

intensity'. This is done by deriving the 'autonomous' trade volume after controlling for the above-mentioned fundamentals using the information included in the estimated fixed effects. These fixed effects were corrected for the estimated impact of FTAs shown in the second step of the regression, as the high absolute value of these coefficients is likely to reflect the high degree of trade integration of countries establishing a free trade area. A high (adjusted) FE for a country pair corresponds to high autonomous trade openness – given the economic and geographical fundamentals – while a low FE indicates a rather closed economy.

In order to get a measure of the average degree of integration into the world economy, the (adjusted) country-pair fixed effects for each country are aggregated across all trading partners. More formally, from the second-step regression, the residuals, which correspond to the fixed effects from the first-step regression after accounting for the impact of the time-invariant gravity fundamentals (such as distance), are aggregated for each country, h, into a measure of trade intensity (ti_h):

$$ti_h = \frac{1}{2(N-1)} \left(\sum_{i=1}^{N-1} \hat{\mu}_{ih}^* + \sum_{j=1}^{N-1} \hat{\mu}_{hj}^* \right)$$

This measure represents an alternative and novel measure of trade intensity that differs from other measures, such as the ratios of exports and imports to GDP or a country's world market share. The difference stems from the fact that the present measure takes into account the geographical location and the size of the country and its trading partners (together with various idiosyncratic characteristics). Accordingly, it helps identify whether, for instance, the small open economies – which are commonly found to have a high trade to GDP ratio – are indeed well integrated into the world economy.

Figure 2.5 ranks the 'overall (global) trade intensity indicators', with more integrated countries on the bottom and less integrated countries on the top. It shows that there is a high degree of heterogeneity across countries in terms of trade intensity. Moreover, for individual countries and regions, this ranking provides several interesting insights.

(1) The industrialised countries tend to display above-average external trade intensity. For example, the United States, South Korea, Japan and Germany trade about two to three times more than an average country in our sample, after controlling for the relevant fundamentals (computed as the exponential of the indicator minus one). This finding also provides more solid evidence that these countries are global export champions, also after controlling for their economic size and

geographic location. For some countries on the bottom (such as the Netherlands), however, the indicator may be upwardly biased given the transit trade accounts for a substantial part of the trade flows. Exceptions among the industrialised countries in term of trade integration are Luxembourg and Greece, which appear to face a somewhat higher level of overall trade resistance. In the case of Luxembourg, however, this may be due to the specific structure of the economy.

(2) Among emerging market economies, it is mainly the south-east Asian countries that show a high degree of external trade intensity – particularly South Korea, Hong Kong and Singapore. Only the Philippines stands out as a country in the region that is less integrated into the world economy. These findings appear relatively intuitive, as it is well known that the countries in south-east Asia are very open to external trade and have very strong trade connections with the rest of the world.

(3) More surprisingly, in spite of the continuation of the transition process, China – given its size and location – is found to be already well integrated into the world economy. Among the Asian countries, China is even more integrated into the global economy than Malaysia, Thailand and Indonesia, albeit less so than Japan and the 'tiger economies' of Hong Kong, South Korea and Singapore. This may partly reflect that the importance of process trade in the case of China, which implies that the domestic value added of China's exports might be relatively low.

(4) At the other end of the spectrum are many transition economies in central and eastern europe, which – in spite of being small open economies – are less integrated by far into the world economy. Only the Czech Republic, Hungary and Poland show a degree of trade intensity that is fairly close to the sample average, while Slovenia trades more than 20 per cent less than an average country, the Slovak Republic and Estonia about 35–45 per cent below the average, and Lithuania and Latvia about 50–70 per cent below the average. On top of the spectrum are the Balkan countries, suggesting that these countries still have significant potential to integrate more into the world economy. For instance, Bosnia-Herzegovina and Albania reach only 18 per cent and 10 per cent of the average autonomous trade level, respectively.

3.5   Bilateral trade intensity: CEEC

To examine the bilateral trade linkages of the CEEC in more detail, an indicator of 'bilateral trade intensity' needs to be contrasted with the 'overall trade intensity' of a country presented in the previous section. The bilateral 'trade indicator' is computed, by analogy to the overall trade indicator as the autonomous trade volume *between each individual country in the sample and the CEEC region* after controlling for the above-mentioned fundamentals. If the *bilateral* indicator is lower than the *overall* indicator, one may argue that the trade potential is not fully exhausted and that there are favourable prospects for further integration.

An example is useful to illustrate this approach: for Germany, the previous section's results (figure 2.5) suggested that it is a very open economy (given its fundamentals) and, therefore, is well integrated overall with the world economy as a whole. Accordingly, the finding that the *bilateral* trade intensity indicator suggests that Germany is also more integrated with the CEEC than many other countries is not very surprising. As the *overall trade indicator* for Germany is rather similar to the *bilateral (German–CEEC) trade indicator*, one may argue that there is only moderate scope for Germany to increase its trade shares in the CEEC (see figure 2.6). As regards the other euro area countries, the CEEC also seem to be well integrated with Finland, while there is still scope for further integration with more distant countries, such as Portugal. These results suggest that the strong rise in the market share of these countries in euro area external trade mainly reflects their convergence towards their normal degree of trade integration.

Moreover, figure 2.6 suggests that the CEEC are regionally very well integrated among themselves, with some countries of the former Yugoslavia and with some countries of the former Soviet Union (particularly Belarus), which may reflect their common historical trade ties within the Comecon system. By contrast, there seems to be significant scope for trade integration of the CEEC with more distant countries such as Japan, Australia and New Zealand, as well as with the emerging markets in Asia and Latin America.

3.6   Bilateral trade intensity: China

While the results above showed that China is *overall* already well integrated into world markets, the degree of bilateral integration between China and its partners also varies substantially. As in the previous section, the distribution of the average trade intensity of China is compared with the overall trade intensity of each trading partner. This *bilateral* trade intensity indicator with China has been computed for each country, and is ordered in figure 2.7 from high to low integration.

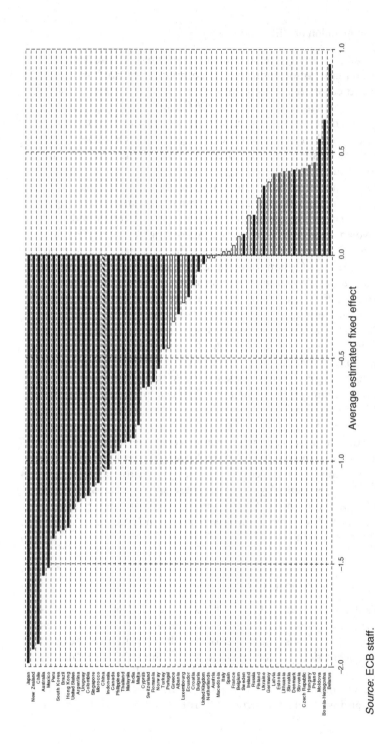

Average estimated fixed effect

Source: ECB staff.

Note: The exponential of each indicator minus one can be interpreted as the multiple of the average degree of integration of each country. White bars indicate euro area countries, grey bars indicate the CEEC and the dashed bar indicates China. Black bars indicate all other countries in the sample.

Figure 2.6   CEEC: indicator of bilateral trade linkages

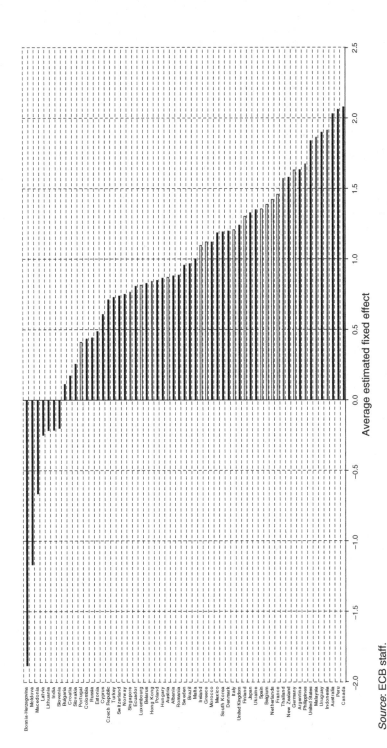

Average estimated fixed effect

Source: ECB staff.
Note: The exponential of each indicator minus one can be interpreted as the multiple of the average degree of integration of each country. White bars indicate euro area countries, grey bars indicate other south-east Asian trading partners. Black bars indicate all other countries in the sample.

Figure 2.7 China: indicator of bilateral trade linkages

In terms of bilateral trade linkages, figure 2.7 suggests that China is very well integrated with industrial countries such as Canada, Australia and the United States and with several Latin American countries (Peru, Uruguay and Argentina). These countries are even more integrated with China than most of the emerging economies in Asia (including Japan). For Canada, Australia and the Latin American countries, this may reflect their specialisation in certain commodities in combination with the strong Chinese demand for raw materials.

While China is also regionally well integrated within Asia, it is somewhat surprising that Singapore and Hong Kong are to be found towards the upper side of the spectrum and, thus, below the average trade integration of China. This finding requires cautious interpretation, however, as it may reflect the fact that for China, Hong Kong and Singapore a common language dummy has been included (and for Hong Kong also a common border dummy) in the estimation of the gravity model. As the coefficients estimated for these dummies are rather high, this adds significantly to the trade potential for these country pairs; since the coefficients of these dummies decline for alternative specifications, it may be argued that the effect of having a common border and a common language is overstated in these calculations, shifting Singapore and Hong Kong by construction to the upper side of the spectrum.

Turning to the euro area countries, China seems to be most closely linked to Germany in terms of international trade. It is also rather well integrated with France, the Netherlands, Spain and Belgium, while it shows more limited trade intensity with Luxembourg and Portugal. China also seems to be rather well integrated with the euro area as a whole, reflecting its relatively high degree of integration with some larger countries (Germany, France and Spain). This notwithstanding, given the strong growth dynamics in China and, more generally, the effects of globalisation, it is likely that trade between China and the euro area will continue to increase at a strong pace.

Moreover, consistent with the finding in the previous section, there still seems to be significant potential for China to increase its trade with many of the CEEC. Finally, the location of India in the figure towards the upper end of the spectrum can be reconciled in terms of the political tensions in the past, and suggests that there is significant potential for this country to improve its trade conditions.

4   Conclusions

This chapter has analysed the rapid trade integration that took place from 1995 to 2004 between China and the CEEC and the rest of the world. Estimations from a gravity model augmented with a set of additional variables have shown that our relatively simple model already explains well trade patterns over time and between countries. We suggest that globalisation was an important factor contributing to the rise in global trade in goods. Moreover, we find that China is, overall, well integrated in world markets already. It has strong trade ties with resource-rich countries and countries in the south-east Asian region. At the same time, it still has scope to integrate further with some other regions of the world, especially eastern Europe and some other emerging markets in Asia.

With regard to the CEEC, both the stylised facts and the estimation results show that these countries still seem to have considerable potential to integrate more into the world economy. Trade reorientation from the former eastern European markets towards the main industrialised countries in the global economy was only partly accomplished. While our indicators suggest that trade intensity with major euro area countries is already relatively advanced, we find that there are still very intense trade relationships in the region (given the economic size of these countries). These countries trade heavily with Belarus and some other CEEC. By contrast, significant scope for further trade integration remains with more distant countries, such as Japan and the United States, as well as with the emerging markets in Asia and Latin America.

In view of the progress that the CEEC and China have already made during the transition process in terms of more complete trade integration with the euro area, the model suggests that the potential for further strong gains in export market shares of these countries in the euro area emanating from a continued trade reorientation towards the euro area seems to be diminishing. Nevertheless, their market share in the euro area may continue to rise if the CEEC and China continue to catch up with and grow stronger than the world economy. Moreover, the further relocation of production in the form of FDI into these countries may also contribute to a further deepening of trade links.[9]

Appendix

Data sources

Countries included: Albania, Algeria, Argentina, Australia, Austria, Belarus, Belgium, Bosnia-Herzegovina, Brazil, Bulgaria, Canada, Chile, China, Colombia, Croatia, Cyprus, Czech Republic, Denmark, Ecuador, Estonia, Finland, France, Germany, Greece, Hong Kong, Hungary,

[9] See, for instance, chapter 4 in di Mauro, Anderton, Ernst *et al.* (2005) and Blattner (2005).

India, Indonesia, Ireland, Italy, Japan, Latvia, Lithuania, Luxembourg, Macedonia, Malaysia, Malta, Mexico, Moldova, Morocco, Netherlands, New Zealand, Norway, Peru, Philippines, Poland, Portugal, Romania, Russia, Singapore, Slovak Republic, Slovenia, South Korea, Spain, Sweden, Switzerland, Thailand, Turkey, Ukraine, United Kingdom, United States, Uruguay.

Trade data: IMF *Direction of Trade Statistics* (DOTS).

GDP: IMF *International Financial Statistics* (IFS), line 99b. For Ecuador, data from World Bank *World Development Indicators* (WDI). Data for Greece up to 1994 from WDI. Data for Turkey up to 1985 from WDI. If there was a large discrepancy between World Bank and IMF data, observations have been dropped. This includes Argentina (1980–4), Bulgaria (1985–92), China (1980–1993), Estonia, Latvia, Lithuania (each 1993–5), Moldova (1995), Russia (1993–4) and Ukraine (1993–5). For Albania, Bosnia-Herzegovina, Moldova and Macedonia, data from the European Bank for Reconstruction and Development (EBRD).

Distance: Great circle distances based on MS Encarta World Atlas software.

Exchange rate: IFS line rf. Exchange rates for individual euro area countries were chain-linked with the euro exchange rate upon EMU entry.

Consumer prices: IFS line 64. For Belarus, China, Russia and the Ukraine, inflation rates (IFS line 64.xx) were transformed into price indices.

Industrial producer price: IFS line 63a for the United States.

Real exchange rate: Product of the dollar exchange rate and the ratio of domestic and foreign consumer prices.

Exchange rate volatility: Standard deviation of the month-on-month log changes in the bilateral nominal exchange rate within a year.

Common border: A matrix is available upon request.

Common language: Based on a matrix including the following languages: English (Australia, Canada, India, Ireland, Hong Kong, Malta, New Zealand, Philippines, Singapore, United Kingdom, United States), Spanish (Argentina, Chile, Colombia, Ecuador, Mexico, Peru, Spain, Uruguay, Venezuela), French (Algeria, Belgium, Canada, France, Luxembourg, Morocco, Switzerland), German (Austria, Germany, Luxembourg, Switzerland), Chinese (China, Hong Kong, Singapore), Russian (Belarus, Estonia, Latvia, Lithuania, Moldova, Russia, Ukraine), Dutch (Belgium, Netherlands), Greek (Greece, Cyprus), Arabic (Algeria,

Morocco), Serbo-Croatian (Bosnia-Herzegovina, Croatia, Slovenia), Portuguese (Brazil, Portugal), Swedish (Sweden, Finland), Albanian (Albania, Macedonia), Malay (Malaysia, Singapore).

Free trade agreements: ASEAN (1992): Brunei Darussalam, Cambodia, Indonesia, Laos, Malaysia, Myanmar, Philippines, Singapore, Thailand, Vietnam; CEFTA (Central European Free Trade Agreement) (1994): Bulgaria (1999), Czech Republic, Hungary, Poland, Romania, Slovak Republic, Slovenia (1997); European Union (EU 15) (1980): Austria (1995), Belgium, Denmark, Finland (1995), France, Germany, Greece (1981), Ireland, Italy, Luxembourg, Netherlands, Portugal (1986), Spain (1986), Sweden (1995), United Kingdom; Mercosur (1993): Argentina, Brazil, Paraguay, Uruguay; NAFTA (1988): Canada, Mexico (1993), United States.

Common territory: Includes countries that constituted at some point in the past twenty years a common country. They include (a) former Czechoslovakia (the Czech Republic and the Slovak Republic), (b) the countries of the former Soviet Union (Belarus, Estonia, Latvia, Lithuania, Moldova, Russia and the Ukraine) and (c) the countries of former Yugoslavia (Bosnia-Herzegovina, Croatia, Macedonia and Slovenia).

References

Anderson, J. E., and E. van Wincoop (2003), 'Gravity with Gravitas: A Solution to the Border Puzzle', *American Economic Review*, **93**, 1, 170–92.

Blattner, T. S. (2005), 'What Drives Foreign Direct Investment in Southeast Asia? A Dynamic Panel Approach', mimeo, European Central Bank, Frankfurt.

Bussière, M., J. Fidrmuc and B. Schnatz (2005), 'Trade Integration of Central and Eastern European Countries: Lessons from a Gravity Model', Working Paper no. 545, European Central Bank, Frankfurt.

Bussière, M., and B. Schnatz (2006), 'Evaluating China's Integration in World Trade: A Benchmark Based on a Gravity Model', Working Paper no. 682, European Central Bank, Frankfurt.

Cheng, I.-H., and H. J. Wall (2005), 'Controlling for Heterogeneity in Gravity Models of Trade and Integration', *Federal Reserve Bank of St Louis Review*, **87**, 1, 49–63.

Deardorff, A. V. (1995), 'Determinants of Bilateral Trade: Does Gravity Work in a Neoclassical World?', Working Paper no. 5377, National Bureau of Economic Research, Cambridge, MA.

Di Mauro, F., R. Anderton, E. Ernst, J. Torres, R. Lecat, M. Cassidy, R. Tedeschi, E. Walch, J. Eggelte, K. Wagner, T. S. Blattner, R. A. de Santis, R. Oliveira-Soires, J.-G. Shen, M. Sydow, T. Warmedinger, T. Zumer and E. Breda (2005), 'Competitiveness and the Export Performance of the Euro Area', Occasional Paper no. 30, European Central Bank, Frankfurt.

Egger, P., and M. Pfaffermayr (2003), 'The Proper Panel Econometric Specification of the Gravity Equation: A Three-way Model with Bilateral Interaction Effects', *Empirical Economics*, **28**, 3, 571–80.

Faruqee, H. (2004), 'Measuring the Trade Effects of EMU', Working Paper no. 04/154, International Monetary Fund, Washington, DC.

Hausman, J. A., and W. E. Taylor (1981), 'Panel Data and Unobservable Individual Effects', *Econometrica*, **49**, 6, 1377–98.

Kao, C., and M.-H. Chiang (2000), 'On the Estimation and Inference of Cointegrated Regression in Panel Data', *Advances in Econometrics*, **15**, 179–222.

Micco, A., E. Stein and G. Ordoñez (2003), 'The Currency Union Effect on Trade: Early Evidence from EMU', *Economic Policy*, **18**, 315–56.

3 Patterns and determinants of production fragmentation in world manufacturing trade

Prema-chandra Athukorala and Nobuaki Yamashita[1]

1 Introduction

International production fragmentation – the geographic separation of activities involved in producing a good (or service) across two or more countries – has been an important feature of the deepening structural interdependence of the world economy in recent decades.[2] After a modest start in electronics and clothing industries in the late 1960s, international production networks have gradually evolved and spread into many industries, such as sport footwear, automobiles, televisions and radio receivers, sewing machines, office equipment, electrical machinery, power and machine tools, cameras and watches. At the formative stage, outsourcing predominantly involved locating small fragments of the production process in a low-cost country and reimporting the assembled components to be incorporated in the final product. Over time, production networks have begun to encompass many countries, resulting in multiple border crossings on the part of unfinished parts before the completion of the final product.

In the early stages of the international fragmentation of production, the processes normally involved a multinational enterprise (MNE) building a subsidiary abroad to perform some of the functions that it once did at home (Helleiner, 1973). Over the years, MNE subsidiaries have begun to subcontract some activities to local (host-country) firms, to which they provide detailed specifications and even fragments of their own technology. Moreover, many MNEs in electronics and related industries have begun to rely increasingly on independent contract manufacturers for the operation of their global-scale production networks – a process that has been facilitated by the standardisation of some components and by advances in modular technology (Sturgeon, 2003; Brown and Linden, 2005).

[1] Research School of Pacific and Asian Studies, Australian National University, and Faculty of Economics and Finance, La Trobe University.
[2] This phenomenon has gone under alternative names, such as 'vertical specialisation', 'slicing the value chain', 'international production sharing' and 'outsourcing'.

At the same time, many firms that are not part of MNE networks have begun to procure components globally through arm's-length trade. All the above developments suggest that an increase in fragmentation-based trade may or may not be accompanied by an increase in the host-country stock of FDI (Brown *et al.*, 2004: 305).

International production fragmentation has resulted in the rapid growth of trade in parts and components ('middle products' or 'fragments of final goods'), at a rate exceeding that of trade in final goods, because parts cross borders, on average, several times before the process is completed. This chapter aims to examine the patterns and determinants of this new form of trade, which is directly related to production fragmentation: what we call 'fragmentation trade'. The analysis concentrates on east Asian countries. To examine such an experience in the wider global context, comparisons are made with two other regional groupings: the North American Free Trade Agreement area and the European Union. The study is based on a new data set extracted from the UN trade database, which distinguishes trade in parts and components from total trade

There is a vast literature based on the standard trade data analysis (which is essentially based on the traditional notion of a horizontal specialisation scenario, in which trade is essentially an exchange of goods that are produced from start to finish in just one country) that unequivocally points to a persistent increase in intra-regional trade in east Asia (both including and excluding Japan) from about the early 1980s (e.g. Kwan, 2001, Drysdale and Garnaut, 1997, Frankel and Wei, 1997, and Petri, 1993). This evidence figures prominently in the current debate on forming regional trading arrangements covering some or all countries in east Asia. In this chapter we argue that, in a context in which component trade is growing rapidly, the standard trade flow analysis can lead to misleading inferences as to the nature and extent of trade integration among countries, for two reasons. First, in the presence of production fragmentation, the trade data overestimate underlying economic activity because goods in process may cross international borders several times before being embodied in the final product. Thus, the total amount of trade recorded could be a multiple of the value of the final goods. Second, and perhaps more importantly, the trade share calculated using reported data can lead to wrong inferences as to the relative importance of the 'region' and the rest of the world for the growth dynamism of a given country/region, even controlling for double-counting in trade. This is because 'fragmentation trade' and trade in related final goods ('final trade') are unlikely to follow the same patterns. Certainly there is ample evidence from the case study literature on multinational enterprises operating in the east Asian region that the demand for the final products comes predominantly from the rest of the world, particularly from North America and countries in the European Union (eg. Borrus, 1997, Dobson and Chia, 1997, and McKendrick *et al.*, 2000).

This chapter relates to, and builds on, Ng and Yeats (2001) and Athukorala (2005). Compared to these studies, the present chapter offers both more current and detailed information on the nature, trends and patterns of fragmentation trade. Its major novelty is in the analysis of the determinants of fragmentation trade, however; to the best of our knowledge, this is the first analysis of the determinants of parts and component trade in a large sample of bilateral trade relations at the global level.[3] Although essentially empirical by design, our analysis is carried out in the context of the existing body of theoretical literature.[4]

The chapter is organised as follows. After a brief presentation of the data set, section 2 examines the nature and extent of global trade in components and east Asia's role in this form of trade specialisation. This section also deals with the implications of the rapid expansion of production fragmentation for analysing the intra- and extra-regional patterns of economic integration of east Asia (and provides a comparison with the European Union and NAFTA). Section 3 uses a 'modified' gravity model to examine the determinants of bilateral trade in parts and components and compare the results with those for trade in final goods (reported trade – parts and components). The final section presents the key inferences.

2   Data source and method of data compilation

There are two approaches to quantifying the magnitude and patterns of manufacturing trade that can be directly attributed to production fragmentation. The first approach, which was commonly used by early studies in this area, uses the records kept by OECD countries (in particular the United States and countries in the European Union) in connection with the special tariff provisions provided for the overseas processing and assembly of domestically produced components – 'outward processing trade (OPT) statistics'. The OPT schemes cover only a selected list of products, however, and the actual product coverage varies significantly not just between countries but within a given country over time.

---

[3] A few studies have examined the implications of production fragmentation for trade patterns with a specific regional (rather than global) focus, including Egger and Egger (2003, 2005), Görg (2000) and Baldone *et al.* (2001).

[4] Important contributions to the theory of production fragmentation include Arndt (1997), Jones (2000), Grossman and Helpman (2005), Jones and Kierzkowski (1990, 2001), Venables (1999) and Yi (2003).

Moreover, and perhaps more importantly, the importance of these tariff concessions as a factor in promoting global sourcing (and therefore the actual utilisation of these schemes) has been significantly diminished over the years by the processes of investment and trade liberalisation and by regional economic integration agreements. The second approach, followed in this chapter, provides a much more comprehensive and consistent coverage of fragmentation trade, as it delineates trade in parts and components from the related final (assembled) goods using individual-country trade statistics recorded on the basis of the Standard International Trade Classification (SITC) of the United Nations.

We make use of data extracted from the UN trade database based on Revision 3 of the Standard International Trade Classification (SITC, Rev 3). In its original form (SITC, Rev 1), the UN trade data reporting system did not distinguish fragmentation trade (parts and components) from final manufactured goods. The SITC Revision 2, introduced in the late 1970s (but implemented by most countries only in the early 1980s), adopted a more detailed commodity classification, which provided for the separation of parts and components within the machinery and transport sector (SITC 7). There was, however, considerable overlap between some advanced-stage component production/assembly and the assembly of final goods in Revision 2 (Ng and Yeats, 2001). Revision 3, introduced in the mid-1980s, marked a significant improvement over Revision 2. In addition to providing a comprehensive coverage of parts and components in SITC 7, it also separately reports parts and components of some products belonging to SITC 8 (miscellaneous manufactures).

The data for SITC 8 do not seem to capture fragmentation trade fully within that commodity category, however. For instance, for some products such as clothing, furniture, and leather products in which outsourcing is prevalent (and perhaps has been increasing), the related components are recorded under other SITC categories (e.g. pieces of textile, parts of furniture, parts of leather soles). Moreover, there is evidence that international production fragmentation has been spreading beyond SITC 7 and 8 to other product categories, in particular to pharmaceutical and chemical products (falling under SITC 5) and machine tools and various metal products (SITC 6). Assembly activities in software trade have also recorded impressive expansion in recent years. These are lumped together with 'special transactions' under SITC 9. As a consequence, the measurement of trade in parts and components reported in this chapter is, presumably, biased downwards.

We report data from the UN trade database for the period from 1992 to 2005, the most recent year for which trade data are available for all reporting countries. 1992 is used as the starting point because, by this year, countries accounting for over 95 per cent of total world manufacturing trade had adopted the new system. The list was prepared by carefully linking the parts and accessories identified in the United Nations Statistical Division: Classification Registry (http:/unstats.un.org/unsd/cr/ registry) with the five-digit SITC product codes. The list contains a total of 225 five-digit products – 168 products belonging to SITC 7 and fifty-seven belonging to SITC 8.[5] The data are tabulated using importer records, which are considered more appropriate than the corresponding exporter records for analysing trade patterns for a number of reasons (Feenstra *et al.*, 2005). Among the countries covered in this study, Taiwan is not covered in the UN data system and Vietnam has not yet begun to make data available according to the standard UN format. Singapore has not been reporting data on its bilateral trade with Indonesia because of political reasons. In these cases, the data gaps have been filled using the corresponding trading partner records.

3   Trends and patterns of production fragmentation

World trade in parts and components[6] increased from about $527 billion in 1992/3 to over $1,500 billion in 2004/5 (table 3.1, figure 3.1).[7] The share of these products in total world manufacturing exports increased from 20.9 per cent to 24.2 per cent between 1992/3 and 2004/5. Components accounted for nearly a third of the total increment in world manufacturing exports between these two periods.

Developed countries continue to account for the bulk of world component trade (table 3.1, figure 3.2). The developing countries' share increased sharply during this period, however, from 18.6 per cent to 39.9 per cent between 1992/3 and 2004/5. The share of east Asia (including Japan) in total world exports of components rose consistently, from 30.7 per cent in 1992/3 to 42.6 per cent in 2004/5, despite a notable decline in the share accounted for by Japan, the dominant economy in the region, in recent years. The share of developing east Asia (east Asia excluding Japan) increased from 14.1 per cent to 31.5 per cent between these two years. Within the group, all reported countries have recorded increases in world market shares.

---

[5] The list is available from the authors on request.
[6] Henceforth, we usually use the term 'components' in place of 'parts and components', for the sake of brevity.
[7] Throughout the chapter intertemporal comparison calculations are made for the two-year averages relating to the end points of the period under study so as to reduce the impact of year-to-year fluctuations on trade flows.

Table 3.1 *World trade in parts and components (1992/3–2004/5)*[1] *(percentages)*

	Exports		Imports	
	1992/3	2004/5	1992/3	2004/5
East Asia[2]	30.7	42.6	22.4	34.8
Japan	16.6	11.1	3.4	4.2
Developing east Asia[3]	14.1	31.5	18.9	30.6
China	1.2	10.0	2.6	10.8
Hong Kong SAR	1.7	0.9	3.6	5.9
South Korea	2.1	4.5	2.9	2.9
Taiwan	3.3	5.6	2.4	2.8
AFTA 6	5.9	10.4	9.9	10.9
South Asia	0.1	0.3	0.1	0.3
Oceania	0.3	0.3	1.4	0.9
NAFTA	24.8	18.8	27.8	21.8
Mexico	2.4	2.8	2.0	3.6
Mercosur	0.7	0.6	0.7	0.6
Andean Common Market	–	–	–	–
Europe	41.5	35.6	43.2	36.6
EU 15	38.5	30.4	40.1	30.6
Eastern Europe	0.6	3.2	0.6	3.3
Rest of Europe	0.3	0.4	0.3	0.4
World	100	100	100	100
($ billions)	(527)	(1,652)	(527)	(1,651)
Memo items:				
Developed countries	79.9	58.4	79.9	58.4
Developing countries	18.6	39.9	18.6	39.9

Notes: – = data not available.
[1] Two-year averages.
[2] Japan plus developing east Asia.
[3] AFTA 6 (Indonesia, Malaysia, the Philippines, Singapore, Thailand and Vietnam) plus China, Hong Kong SAR (Special Administrative Region), South Korea and Taiwan.
Source: Compiled from UN Comtrade database.

The growing importance of China in component trade is particularly noteworthy. The share of China in total world component exports increased from about 1 per cent to 10 per cent and in total imports from 2.6 per cent to 10.8 per cent between 1992/3 and 2004/5. Contrary to the popular perception of China crowding out the 'rest', this increase has been within an overall increase in exports from other newcomers in the region. For instance, the combined export share of the six main member countries of the ASEAN Free Trade Area (AFTA) more than doubled (from 5.9 per cent to 10.4 per cent) between these two periods.

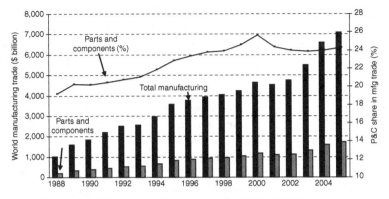

Figure 3.1 World manufacturing trade (1988–2005)

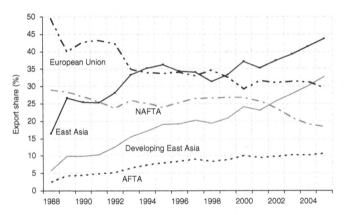

Figure 3.2 Share of parts and components in manufacturing exports by region (1988–2005)

Has the formation of NAFTA and the integration of some of the former Soviet Union countries with the rest of Europe adversely affected developing east Asia's relative position in world assembly activities? Certainly, proximity to industrial countries and relatively low wages by regional standards (though not with respect to some of the east Asian countries) can be considered as added advantages of these countries compared to east Asian countries in production-fragmentation-based international specialisation (Egger and Egger, 2005; Ng and Yeats, 2003; Kierzkowski, 2001). The data do not, however, point to any dampening effect of exports from these countries on the relative world market position of east Asia; the world market shares of Mexico and the rest of Europe (European countries other than the EU 15) have increased, albeit at a much slower rate than that of developing east Asia. It would appear that, in spite of geographical proximity and the tariff concessions of FTAs, US producers still find east Asia a more attractive location for outsourcing. A new dimension of regional production sharing in Europe has been added by the economic integration taking place there.

Table 3.2 presents comparative statistics on the share of parts and components in total manufacturing exports and imports and their contribution to the growth of manufacturing trade from 1992/3 to 2004/5. It is evident that the share of component trade for east Asia as a group is much higher than in all other regions in the world. In 2004/5 components accounted for 30.0 per cent of total manufacturing exports from developing east Asia, compared to the world average of 24.2 per cent. Within east Asia, the countries belonging to AFTA stand out for their heavy dependence on production fragmentation for export dynamism. In 2004/5 components accounted for 40.3 per cent of total manufacturing exports in AFTA, up from 27.5 per cent in 1992/3. Between these two periods, the share of components in total manufacturing exports more than tripled in China, rising from 5.3 per cent to 19.5 per cent. Interestingly, even for Taiwan and South Korea, the relative importance of components in total manufacturing exports (and imports) has increased over the years, contradicting the popular belief that these countries are shifting from component production to final goods production.

Disaggregated data (not reported here for brevity) show that, in all countries/regions, component trade is heavily concentrated in the machinery and transport equipment sector (SITC 7). This sector accounts for over 90 per cent of the combined component trade of SITC 7 and SITC 8 (miscellaneous manufacturing). Within SITC 7, east Asia's component exports and imports are equally heavily concentrated in electronics and electrical industries. Semiconductors and other electronics components (components within SITC 77) alone accounted for some 50 per cent of component exports from east Asia in 2004/5. Adding to these items components for telecommunication equipment (SITC 76) and office and automated data-processing machines (SITC 75) increases the concentration ratio to almost 90 per cent of total exports of components. The balance consists largely of electrical machinery (SITC 77) and automobile parts (SITC 78). The degree of concentration of electronics component trade is much larger in AFTA (over 60 per cent) compared to the regional average. These electronics and electrical products are also the major areas of activity in other countries/regions. The trade patterns of these

Table 3.2 Parts and components (PCs) in manufacturing (Mfg) trade (1992/3–2004/5)

(a) Exports

	Value of PCs ($ billions)		Share of PCs in Mfg exports (%)		Annual average growth of Mfg exports (%)	Annual average growth of PC exports (%)	Contribution of PCs to growth of Mfg exports (%)
	1992/3	2004/5	1992/3	2004/5	1992–2005	1992–2005	1992–2005
East Asia	161.8	703.0	21.9	30.0	9.6	12.5	33.7
Japan	87.5	182.9	26.9	32.9	4.3	6.3	41.4
Developing east Asia	74.3	520.0	18.0	29.1	12.4	16.7	32.4
China	6.1	165.3	5.3	19.5	17.4	29.7	21.7
Hong Kong SAR	8.8	15.2	18.8	27.7	0.6	3.4	79.4
South Korea	11.1	74.3	19.5	31.0	12.2	17.0	34.6
Taiwan	17.3	93.1	21.2	43.5	8.1	14.4	57.2
AFTA 6	31.0	172.1	27.5	40.3	11.6	14.7	44.9
South Asia	0.7	5.0	3.6	6.4	12.1	17.9	7.3
Oceania	1.6	4.2	15.7	15.9	8.1	8.1	16.0
NAFTA	130.7	310.7	29.7	29.8	7.2	7.1	29.9
Mexico	12.7	46.2	38.4	30.2	12.5	10.5	27.9
Mercosur	3.6	10.6	14.6	14.4	9.3	9.0	14.3
Andean Common Market	0.2	0.7	5.0	4.7	11.4	10.7	4.6
Europe	218.5	588.3	18.3	19.6	6.5	6.9	20.5
EU 15	203.0	501.5	18.8	19.6	6.0	6.2	20.2
Eastern Europe	3.1	53.7	11.3	26.3	16.2	24.1	28.6
Rest of Europe	1.6	6.4	15.6	22.5	7.3	9.9	26.4
World	527.0	1652.0	20.9	24.2	7.8	9.0	26.1

Table 3.2 (cont.)

(b) Imports

	Value of PCs ($ billions)		Share of PCs in Mfg imports (%)		Annual average growth of Mfg imports (%)	Annual average growth of PC imports (%)	Contribution of PCs to growth of Mfg imports (%)
	1992/3	2004/5	1992/3	2004/5	1992–2005	1992–2005	1992–2005
East Asia	117.9	573.8	22.9	38.0	9.0	13.1	45.8
Japan	18.1	69.1	16.5	25.9	7.0	10.6	32.5
Developing east Asia	99.8	504.7	24.7	40.6	9.5	13.5	48.3
China	13.4	178.6	17.7	38.8	15.6	21.6	43.0
Hong Kong SAR	18.9	97.7	16.4	37.3	6.9	13.8	53.7
South Korea	15.0	48.2	28.8	32.4	8.3	9.0	34.3
Taiwan	12.7	45.8	29.6	34.4	11.2	13.3	36.7
AFTA 6	52.4	180.2	32.6	48.5	7.2	10.5	60.6
South Asia	0.7	5.0	3.6	6.4	12.1	17.9	7.3
Oceania	7.3	15.0	17.3	13.8	7.6	6.0	11.6
NAFTA	146.8	360.5	24.7	22.5	8.1	7.4	21.2
Mexico	10.7	60.0	23.0	34.1	10.7	13.9	38.1
Mercosur	3.6	10.6	14.6	14.4	9.3	9.0	14.3
Andean Common Market	0.2	0.7	5.0	4.7	11.4	10.7	4.6
Europe	227.5	605.0	18.7	19.9	6.4	6.8	20.7
EU 15	211.4	505.5	19.1	20.3	5.5	5.9	21.3
Eastern Europe	3.1	53.7	11.3	26.3	16.2	24.1	28.6
Rest of Europe	1.6	6.4	15.6	22.5	7.3	9.9	26.4
World	527.0	1651.2	20.9	24.1	7.8	9.0	26.0

Notes: – Data not available.

Source: Compiled from UN Comtrade database.

countries/regions are characterised by a greater presence of other items, however, such as road vehicles (SITC 78) and transport equipment (SITC 79), for which transportation costs are presumably an important consideration for production location. Overall, these differences are consistent with east Asia's competitive edge in component specialisation in electrical and electronic industries.

Table 3.3 compares regional patterns of total manufacturing trade and trade in components. In terms of the conventionally used trade data, intra-regional manufacturing trade (export plus imports) in east Asia is significant and growing rapidly. The share of total intra-regional trade in east Asia increased from 47.3 per cent in 1992/3 to 54 per cent in 2004/5. Intra-regional trade in developing east Asia increased from 37.1 per cent in 1992/3 to 42.6 per cent in 2004/5. For AFTA the magnitude of these figures is much smaller, but they still point to an impressive and persistent increase during this period, from 17.1 per cent to 20.7 per cent. By contrast, the intra-regional trade share declined somewhat (from 66.2 per cent to 59 per cent) in the European Union and increased marginally (from 40 per cent to 40.7 per cent) in NAFTA.

Unlike in the European Union and NAFTA, the east Asian intra-regional trade ratio hides a significant asymmetry in regional trade patterns on the import and export sides. In 2004/5 intra-regional import flows amounted to 68.9 per cent of east Asia's total manufacturing imports, up from 57.8 per cent in 1992/3. The intra-regional share in total regional exports was significantly lower: 40 per cent in 1992/3 and 44.4 per cent in 2004/5. In other words, the region is much more heavily dependent on extra-regional trade for its growth dynamism than is (misleadingly) suggested by the total regional trade share, and this dependence remained virtually unchanged during this period.

This imbalance in intra-regional trade is to a large extent a reflection of the unique nature of Japan's involvement in fragmentation trade in east Asia. Japan's trade relations with the rest of east Asia predominantly take the form of using the region as an assembly base for meeting demand in the region and, more importantly, for exporting to the rest of the world. Japan has persistently maintained a trade surplus with all east Asian countries in both total manufacturing trade and trade in components, of which the latter is much larger (the data are not reported for brevity).

Component trade accounts for a significant and growing share of intra-regional trade in manufacturing in east Asia, on the export and import sides alike. Moreover, the share of components in intra-regional trade is much larger than the comparable figures for the region's extra-regional trade (table 3.4). In 2004/5 components accounted for 60.9 per cent of intra-regional east Asian exports, compared to 44.4 per cent of the

Table 3.3 Direction of manufacturing trade: total manufacturing and parts and components (1992/3 and 2004/5) (percentages)

(a) Exports

Partner			Total manufacturing exports								Parts and components exports							
		EA	Japan	DEA	China +HK	AFTA	NAFTA	EU 15	World	EA	Japan	DEA	China +HK	AFTA	NAFTA	EU 15	World
East Asia (EA)	1992/3	40.0	5.2	34.9	18.5	13.0	32.3	20.3	100	44.0	3.4	40.5	14.5	20.8	33.5	17.6	100
	2004/5	44.4	6.7	37.7	23.2	10.6	26.4	17.7	100	60.9	6.4	54.5	32.5	17.6	19.5	12.8	100
Japan	1992/3	32.5	.	32.5	11.9	14.8	34.8	21.4	100	37.3	.	37.3	10.6	19.4	36.9	18.8	100
	2004/5	42.8	.	42.8	22.2	12.7	27.8	17.1	100	53.0	.	53.0	28.1	18.0	25.2	14.8	100
Developing east Asia (DEA)	1992/3	46.0	9.3	36.7	23.6	11.5	30.4	19.5	100	51.8	7.5	44.3	19.0	22.3	29.5	16.1	100
	2004/5	44.9	8.8	36.1	23.5	9.9	25.9	17.9	100	63.7	8.6	55.1	34.1	17.4	17.4	12.2	100
China+HK	1992/3	50.6	7.7	43.0	36.6	4.7	26.1	19.1	100	64.5	4.9	59.5	41.3	13.2	18.5	12.7	100
	2004/5	38.1	9.7	28.5	14.5	5.7	30.0	20.0	100	58.7	9.1	49.6	20.2	11.9	19.5	13.7	100
AFTA	1992/3	41.0	9.3	31.7	8.5	20.8	33.0	22.3	100	52.4	7.2	45.2	8.9	32.8	29.9	16.7	100
	2004/5	50.2	8.7	41.4	19.1	19.4	22.6	17.2	100	65.1	8.0	57.1	27.2	26.1	16.1	13.2	100
South Asia	1992/3	18.3	6.2	12.1	5.7	5.4	32.0	40.3	100	29.4	2.8	26.6	3.4	22.3	16.6	34.2	100
	2004/5	17.5	2.0	15.5	8.7	5.6	29.2	32.7	100	20.2	3.5	16.7	6.0	9.4	26.8	33.2	100
Oceania	1992/3	43.2	9.6	33.6	8.9	20.1	16.3	13.9	100	40.3	8.9	31.4	5.7	20.5	21.5	24.3	100
	2004/5	28.6	4.7	23.9	9.6	10.2	19.4	15.5	100	34.2	2.2	32.0	8.2	16.4	22.0	18.6	100
NAFTA	1992/3	20.7	7.5	13.2	3.9	6.3	46.9	22.0	100	21.3	6.7	14.6	3.0	8.2	47.8	23.3	100
	2004/5	17.2	4.5	12.6	5.1	5.1	51.5	18.7	100	24.7	5.0	19.7	5.9	10.6	47.8	18.0	100
EU 15	1992/3	8.1	2.5	5.5	2.2	2.5	9.7	66.9	100	7.5	1.3	6.2	2.0	3.3	12.0	66.1	100
	2004/5	7.8	1.9	6.0	3.3	1.8	11.3	58.2	100	11.0	1.5	9.5	4.7	3.7	11.2	56.5	100
World	1992/3	20.3	4.3	16.0	7.6	6.4	23.6	43.8	100	22.3	3.3	18.9	6.1	9.9	27.8	40.1	100
	2004/5	22.0	3.9	18.1	10.5	5.4	23.3	36.4	100	34.7	4.2	30.6	16.7	11.0	21.8	30.6	100

Table 3.3 (*cont.*)

(b) *Imports*

Partner		Total manufacturing imports								Parts and components imports							
		EA	Japan	DEA	China +HK	AFTA	NAFTA	EU 15	World	EA	Japan	DEA	China +HK	AFTA	NAFTA	EU 15	World
East Asia	1992/3	57.8	20.6	37.1	16.0	9.0	17.8	17.0	100	60.7	27.8	32.9	8.4	13.8	23.7	13.0	100
	2004/5	68.9	15.8	53.1	22.8	14.2	11.9	13.3	100	74.6	16.9	57.7	21.2	19.5	13.4	9.6	100
Japan	1992/3	35.6	.	35.6	11.6	9.7	30.6	25.4	100	32.0	.	32.0	5.3	12.9	50.4	15.3	100
	2004/5	58.8	.	58.8	32.9	14.1	17.8	17.9	100	64.9	.	64.9	46.5	19.9	22.4	10.8	100
Developing east Asia	1992/3	63.7	26.1	37.6	17.2	8.8	14.4	14.8	100	65.7	32.7	33.0	8.9	14.0	19.1	12.6	100
	2004/5	71.0	19.1	51.9	20.7	14.3	10.6	12.3	100	75.9	19.2	56.7	17.7	19.5	12.1	9.4	100
China+HK	1992/3	71.3	20.3	51.0	30.9	5.0	8.9	12.2	100	72.4	28.8	43.7	19.1	8.5	12.0	12.6	100
	2004/5	75.2	17.1	58.1	18.2	11.3	7.4	11.7	100	82.8	18.6	64.2	13.2	17.0	6.7	8.5	100
AFTA	1992/3	59.6	30.0	29.6	4.7	14.6	17.3	16.7	100	64.1	32.4	31.7	3.8	19.4	20.4	13.0	100
	2004/5	66.4	19.0	47.4	13.8	22.2	14.4	12.7	100	68.2	18.2	50.0	11.9	24.9	18.3	10.2	100
South Asia	1992/3	31.6	11.2	20.4	6.8	5.6	13.0	39.5	100	35.4	22.0	13.4	3.4	6.4	18.1	39.1	100
	2004/5	39.7	6.0	33.7	15.7	9.9	10.7	29.7	100	44.6	7.9	36.7	13.4	14.4	14.7	32.1	100
Oceania	1992/3	39.5	21.0	18.4	6.2	5.2	24.4	24.2	100	34.0	22.1	11.9	2.6	3.7	36.1	24.0	100
	2004/5	44.8	13.6	31.1	15.9	9.2	17.6	25.1	100	36.9	11.9	25.0	9.1	10.1	28.7	25.4	100
NAFTA	1992/3	40.2	19.0	21.2	7.1	6.3	34.8	17.7	100	36.9	22.0	14.9	1.9	6.3	42.6	16.7	100
	2004/5	38.6	9.7	29.0	17.0	6.1	33.7	18.1	100	38.0	12.8	25.2	9.8	7.7	41.3	15.6	100
EU 15	1992/3	13.6	6.3	7.3	2.8	2.3	8.8	65.5	100	13.4	7.8	5.6	0.9	2.4	14.4	63.5	100
	2004/5	16.6	3.8	12.8	7.2	3.0	7.8	59.8	100	17.9	5.3	12.5	4.9	4.5	11.1	56.1	100
World	1992/3	29.3	12.9	16.4	6.4	4.5	17.5	42.9	100	30.7	16.6	14.1	2.8	5.9	24.8	38.5	100
	2004/5	34.2	8.1	26.1	13.2	6.2	15.2	37.4	100	42.5	11.1	31.5	10.9	10.4	18.8	30.3	100

Table 3.3 (cont.)

(c) *Total manufacturing trade (export + imports)*

Partner:	Year	Total manufacturing trade								Parts and components trade							
		EA	Japan	DEA	China +HK	AFTA	NAFTA	EU 15	World	EA	Japan	DEA	China +HK	AFTA	NAFTA	EU 15	World
East Asia	1992/3	47.3	11.5	35.8	17.5	11.3	26.4	19.0	100	51.0	13.7	37.3	11.9	17.9	29.4	15.6	100
	2004/5	54.0	10.2	43.7	23	12.0	20.7	16.0	100	67.1	11.1	56.0	27.4	18.5	16.7	11.4	100
Japan	1992/3	33.2	·	33.2	11.8	13.6	33.7	22.4	100	36.4	·	36.4	9.7	18.3	39.1	18.2	100
	2004/5	48.0	·	48	25.6	13.2	24.6	17.4	100	56.3	·	56.3	33.1	18.5	24.4	13.7	100
Developing east Asia	1992/3	54.7	17.6	37.1	20.5	10.2	22.5	17.2	100	59.8	21.9	37.8	13.2	17.6	23.5	14.1	100
	2004/5	55.6	13.0	42.6	22.3	11.7	19.6	15.6	100	69.7	13.8	55.9	26	18.4	14.8	10.8	100
China+HK	1992/3	61.8	14.5	47.3	33.5	4.8	16.8	15.4	100	69.9	21.2	48.7	26.1	10.0	14.0	12.6	100
	2004/5	54.6	13.0	41.6	16.2	8.2	20	16.3	100	73.3	14.9	58.4	16	15.0	11.8	10.5	100
AFTA	1992/3	51.9	21.5	30.4	6.3	17.1	23.8	19.0	100	59.7	23.1	36.7	5.7	24.3	23.9	14.4	100
	2004/5	57.7	13.5	44.2	16.7	20.7	18.8	15.1	100	66.7	13.2	53.5	19.4	25.5	17.2	11.7	100
South Asia	1992/3	24.6	8.6	16	6.2	5.5	23.0	39.9	100	34.2	18.2	16.1	3.4	9.6	17.8	38.1	100
	2004/5	28.0	3.9	24.1	12.0	7.6	20.5	31.3	100	36.8	6.5	30.3	11.1	12.8	18.5	32.4	100
Oceania	1992/3	40.2	18.8	21.4	6.7	8.1	22.9	22.2	100	35.2	19.8	15.4	3.1	6.7	33.5	24.0	100
	2004/5	41.6	11.9	29.7	14.6	9.4	17.9	23.2	100	36.3	9.7	26.6	8.9	11.5	27.3	24.0	100
NAFTA	1992/3	31.9	14.1	17.8	5.7	6.3	40.0	19.5	100	29.6	14.8	14.8	2.4	7.2	45.0	19.8	100
	2004/5	30.2	7.6	22.5	12.3	5.7	40.7	18.3	100	31.8	9.2	22.7	8.0	9.1	44.3	16.7	100
EU 15	1992/3	10.9	4.4	6.4	2.5	2.4	9.2	66.2	100	10.5	4.6	5.9	1.4	2.9	13.3	64.7	100
	2004/5	12.2	2.8	9.4	5.2	2.4	9.6	59.0	100	14.4	3.4	11.0	4.8	4.1	11.1	56.3	100
World	1992/3	24.8	8.6	16.2	7.0	5.4	20.5	43.4	100	26.5	10.0	16.5	4.5	7.9	26.3	39.3	100
	2004/5	28.1	6.0	22.1	11.9	5.8	19.3	36.9	100	38.6	7.6	31.0	13.8	10.7	20.3	30.5	100

Source: Compiled from UN Comtrade database using the commodity/country classification described in section 3.

Table 3.4 *Intra-regional trade shares: total manufacturing, parts and components and final trade (1992/3 and 2004/5) (percentages)*

		East Asia	Developing east Asia	AFTA	NAFTA	EU 15
Total Manufacturing						
Exports (X)	1992/3	40.0	36.7	20.8	46.9	66.9
	2004/5	44.4	36.1	19.4	51.5	58.2
Imports (M)	1992/3	57.8	37.6	14.6	34.8	65.5
	2004/5	68.9	51.9	22.2	33.7	59.8
Trade (X+M)	1992/3	47.3	37.1	17.1	40.0	66.2
	2004/5	54.0	42.6	20.7	40.7	59.0
Parts and components						
Exports	1992/3	44.0	44.3	32.8	47.8	66.1
	2004/5	60.9	55.1	26.1	47.8	56.5
Imports	1992/3	60.7	33.0	19.4	42.6	63.5
	2004/5	74.6	56.7	24.9	41.3	56.1
Trade (X+M)	1992/3	51.0	37.8	24.3	45.0	64.7
	2004/5	67.1	55.9	25.5	44.3	56.3
Final goods						
Exports	1992/3	38.9	35.1	16.2	46.5	67.0
	2004/5	37.3	28.3	14.8	53.1	58.7
Imports	1992/3	56.9	39.0	12.2	32.3	66.0
	2004/5	65.3	48.6	19.7	31.5	60.7
Trade (X+M)	1992/3	46.2	37.0	13.9	38.1	66.5
	2004/5	47.5	35.8	16.9	39.5	59.7

Source: Compiled from UN Comtrade database.

region's total manufacturing exports. The significance of component trade looms even larger for developing east Asia, and in particular for the member countries of AFTA. South Korea and Taiwan are also involved in sizeable cross-border trade with the other countries in the region. For all east Asian countries, the share of components in both intra-regional exports and imports has increased at a much faster rate than in exports to and imports from countries outside the region.

So far we have noted two important peculiarities of the trade patterns in east Asia compared to total global trade and the trade of the European Union and NAFTA. First, component trade has played a much more important role in trade expansion in east Asia relative to the overall global experience and the experiences of the countries in other major regions. Second, trade in components accounts for a much larger share in intra-regional trade compared to the region's trade with the rest of the world. Given these two peculiarities, trade flow analysis based on reported trade data is bound to yield a misleading picture as to the relative importance of intra-regional trade relations (as against global trade) in the growth dynamism of east Asia (and for AFTA and other subregional groupings therein). The data reported in table 3.4 on intra-regional shares of trade in total manufacturing, components and final goods for various regional economic groupings help us understand this important point.

The intra-regional share of final manufacturing trade in east Asia increased only marginally, from 46.2 per cent to 47.5 per cent, between 1992/3 and 2004/5, in sharp contrast to a notable increase (from 47.3 per cent to 54 per cent) recorded by the conventionally used trade share (which covers both components and final goods). While the difference between intra-regional shares of final and total trade is observable for both exports and imports, the magnitude of the difference is much larger on the export side. The difference in magnitude between the regional trade shares estimated in gross and net terms is much larger for developing east Asia and ASEAN compared to estimates for the entire region. In 2004/5 only 28 per cent of final goods exports from developing Asia found markets within the region, compared to 36.1 per cent of total exports. For AFTA the relevant figures were 14.8 per cent and 19.7 per cent, respectively. It is also interesting to note that, unlike in the case of east Asia (or developing east Asia and AFTA), the estimated intra-regional trade shares for NAFTA, the European Union and the other regional groupings are remarkably resilient to the inclusion or exclusion of component trade.

In sum, the estimates presented in this section support the hypothesis that, in a context in which fragmentation trade is expanding rapidly, the standard trade flows analysis can lead to misleading inferences regarding the ongoing process of economic integration through trade. Production fragmentation leads to the double-counting of trade flows in published trade data, because goods in process cross international borders several times in the course of their production sequence. The total amount of trade involving the goods while in process can be a multiple of the final value of that good. Moreover, trade shares calculated using reported data can lead to wrong inferences as to the relative importance of the 'region' and the rest of the world for the growth dynamism of a given country/region, even controlling for double-counting in trade. When data on component trade are excluded from trade flows, our estimates suggest that extra-regional trade is much more important than intra-regional trade for the continued growth dynamism of east Asia, both including and excluding Japan. This is because the rate of expansion of component trade depends crucially on the demand for the related final goods.

4   Determinants of fragmentation trade

We now turn to a more formal examination of the determinants of inter-country/inter-regional differences in the growth of fragmentation trade. The analytical tool used for this purpose is a gravity model, which has established itself in the empirical trade literature as the most successful model for sorting out the relative importance of geographical factors versus economic factors in explaining trade patterns. We augment the basic gravity model by incorporating a number of explanatory variables suggested by recent theoretical and empirical advances in the emerging literature on international production fragmentation. Our specification of the gravity model is:

$$
\begin{aligned}
\ln M_{i,j} = \alpha &+ \beta_1 \ln GDP_i + \beta_2 \ln GDP_j + \beta_3 \ln PGDP_i + \beta_4 \ln PGDP_j \\
&+ \beta_5 \ln |\Delta PGDP_{i,j}| + \beta_6 \ln DST_{i,j} + \beta_7 LNG_{i,j} + \beta_8 BRD_{i,j} \\
&+ \beta_9 RWG_{i,j} + \beta_{10} RTAINT_{i,j} + \beta_{11} RTAEXT_{i,j} + \beta_{12} AFTAINT_{i,j} \\
&+ \beta_{13} AFTAEXT_{i,j} + \gamma T + \varepsilon_{ij}
\end{aligned}
$$

Subscripts i and j refer to the importing and exporting country in a bilateral trade relation, and the variables are listed and defined below, with the postulated sign of the regression coefficient for the explanatory variables in brackets.

M	Bilateral trade between i and j, measured as imports of country i coming from country j.
GDP	Real gross domestic product, a measure of the economic size (+).
$PGDP$	Real GDP per capita (+).
$|\Delta PGDP|$	Absolute difference in GDP per capita (+).
DST	The distance between i and j (−).
LNG	A dummy variable that is unity if i and j have a common language and zero otherwise (+).
BRD	A dummy variable that is unity if i and j share the same border (+).
RWG	Manufacturing wages of i relative to those of j (+).
$RTAINT$	A dummy that is unity if both i and j belong to the same regional trade agreement (+).
$RTAEXT$	A dummy, taking unity when only i belongs to an RTA (− or +).
$AFTAINT$	A dummy, which is unity if both i and j are members of AFTA (+).
$AFTAEXT$	A dummy, taking unity when only i belongs to $AFTA$ (− or +).

T	A set of time dummy variables to capture year-specific 'fixed' effects.
α	A constant term.
ε	A stochastic error term, representing the omitted other influences on bilateral trade.

The use of GDP as an explanatory variable of bilateral trade flows is normally justified by the modern theory of trade under imperfect competition (the monopolistic competition model of trade): one will choose to trade more with a large country than with a small country because it has more variety to offer. The use of this variable is also consistent with the theory of international production fragmentation, which predicts that the optimal degree of fragmentation depends on the size of the market because the scale of production would determine the length to which such division of labour can proceed (Jones et al., 2004). The size of GDP can also be treated as a proxy for the 'market thickness' (the economic depth of trading nations), which impacts positively on the location of outsourcing activity (Grossman and Helpman, 2005). There are also reasons to believe that GDP per capita has a positive effect over and above the effect of GDP; as countries grow richer, the scale of the output from industries becomes conducive to fragmentation. In addition, more developed countries have better ports and communication systems, which facilitate trade by reducing the cost of maintaining the 'service links' involved in vertical specialisation.[8] The choice of absolute difference in per capita GDP as an explanatory variable is based on the premise that a pair of countries with dissimilar levels of per capita GDP are more likely to trade with each other than a pair with similar levels – which is why the expected sign is positive (Helpman, 1987).

Relative labour costs (measured as relative manufacturing wages – *RWG* – adjusted for exchange rate differential) is presumably a major factor impacting on the global spread of fragmentation-based (vertical) specialisation (Jones, 2000). Another important determinant of trade flows suggested by the theory of production fragmentation is the cost of service links (Jones 2000). There is no single measure of such costs. We can hypothesise, as mentioned above, that GDP per capita has a positive effect over and above the effect of GDP, with the scale of industrial output

---

[8] Following Egger and Egger (2005), in experimental runs we included two infrastructure variables: main telephone lines per 1,000 people (*TELE*) and electricity production in kilowatts (*ELET*). They were dropped from the final estimates because they were found to be highly correlated with *PGDP*. It seems that there is no need for additional variables specifically to capture infrastructure quality, as it is closely correlated with the stage of development as measured by *PGDP*.

becoming conducive to fragmentation as countries become wealthier and more developed, in turn leading to the construction of better ports and communication systems that facilitate trade by lowering the cost of maintaining such service links. We also include three additional variables to capture the cost of service links: distance (*DST*), a common border dummy (*BRD*) and a common language dummy (*LNG*). In the standard gravity model, distance (*DST*) is included as a proxy for transport (shipping) costs and other costs associated with time lags, such as internet charges and spoilage, as well as costs associated with physical distance, such as ignorance of foreign customs and tastes.[9]

Distance can, in fact, be a more important influence on component trade than on final trade, because of the multiple border crossings involved in the value added chain. A country with better infrastructure (such as well-established broadband networking) is presumably a preferable location of global sourcing because of the lower cost of establishing service links. The common border dummy (*BRD*) is included to capture possible additional advantages of proximity that are not captured by the standard distance measure (the great circle distance between capital cities). A common language dummy (*LNG*) is included to capture the possibility that the use of a common language can facilitate trade by reducing transaction costs and by generating a better understanding of each other's culture and legal systems.

We include regional dummy variables *RTAINT* and *RTAEXT* to capture the possible trade effects of membership in four regional trading agreements (AFTA, the European Union, NAFTA and Mercosur), with all countries not belonging to any RTAs forming the base group.[10] Two additional dummy variables for AFTA, defined in the same manner, are included to capture the special historical role played by AFTA countries (in particular Malaysia, Thailand and the Philippines) in international production networks compared to other RTA member countries (Athukorala, 2005).

Component trade is postulated to be more sensitive to tariff changes (whether in the context of an RTA or otherwise) than is final trade (or total trade as captured in published trade data) (Yi, 2003). Normally a tariff is

---

[9] Technological advances during the post-war era have certainly contributed to a 'death of distance' (*à la* Cairncross, 1997) when it comes to international communication costs. There is evidence, however, that the geographical 'distance' is still a key factor in determining international transport costs, in particular shipping costs (Hummels, 2001).

[10] In experimental runs we tested separate dummies for each RTA, but eventually we collapsed them into a single dummy (with an AFTA dummy added) because we found that there were no statistically significant differences in the magnitude of individual coefficients other than that for AFTA.

incurred each time a good in process crosses a border. Consequently, with a one percentage point reduction in tariff, the cost of production of a vertically integrated good declines by a multiple of this initial reduction, in contrast to a one percentage point decline in the cost of a regular traded good. Moreover, a tariff reduction may make it more profitable for goods previously produced in their entirety in one country now to become vertically specialised. Consequently, the trade-stimulating effect of an RTA would be higher for parts and components trade than for normal trade, other things remaining unchanged. In the case of fragmentation trade, however, one can assume a positive coefficient, because any positive effect from an RTA on the depth of regional outsourcing has the potential to promote such activities extra-regionally as well (assuming that there are 'rules or origin' built into the RTA). Finally, the time-specific fixed effects (T) are included to control for general technological change and other time-varying factors.

The model is estimated using annual bilateral trade data for forty-one countries over the period from 1992 to 2004.[11] The trade data relate to the 'machinery and transport equipment' section of the UN Standard International Trade Classification system (SITC 7). The prime focus of the analysis is on trade in components. We also estimate the model for final goods trade (reported trade minus vertical trade) for the purposes of comparison, however. Under each category, bilateral trade based on given reporting countries' imports (rather than using a composite trade variable as the dependent variable, as is commonly done in trade flow analysis based on the gravity model) is estimated in order to allow for possible differences in the nature/magnitude of the postulated impact of a given explanatory variable on bilateral trade flows. We have used a random effect estimator as our preferred estimation technique. The alternative fixed effect estimator is not appropriate, because our model contains a number of time-invariant variables (distance, language, border and RTA dummies) that are central to our analysis of fragmentation-based trade. There is nevertheless a major limitation to the random effect estimator compared to its fixed effect counterpart, in that it can yield inconsistent and biased estimates if the unobserved fixed effects are correlated with the remaining component of the error term. This is unlikely to be a serious problem in our case, however, because N (the number of explanatory variables) is larger than T (the number of 'within' observations) (Wooldridge, 2001). The random effect estimator also takes care of the serial correlation problem. The results are reported

---

[11] The data set includes all countries that accounted for at least 0.1 per cent of total world manufacturing exports in 2000/1.

Table 3.5 *Determinants of world trade in machinery and transport equipment (SITC 7): regression results (1992–2003)*[1]

Explanatory variables[2]	Parts and components		Final goods	
	Coefficient	SE	Coefficient	SE
Log GDP, importer	0.984	0.127[a]	0.875	0.090[a]
Log GDP, exporter	0.915	0.029[a]	0.979	0.023[a]
Log per capita GDP, importer	0.328	0.126[a]	0.248	0.105[b]
Log per capita GDP, exporter	0.357	0.036[a]	0.361	0.036[a]
Log absolute per capita GDP differences	0.055	0.041	0.078	0.039[b]
Log relative labour cost (*RWG*)[3]	0.544	0.093[a]	0.164	0.078[b]
Log distance (*DST*)	−0.970	0.073[a]	−1.070	0.063[a]
Common language dummy (*LNG*)	0.931	0.121[a]	0.656	0.109[a]
Common land border dummy (*BRD*)	0.206	0.180	0.054	0.160
RTA dummies				
Intra-RTA trade (*RTAINT*)[4]	−0.122	0.380	−0.032	0.284
Extra-RTA trade of RTA member countries (*RTAEXT*)	−0.239	0.373	−0.187	0.290
Intra-AFTA trade (*AFTAINT*)[5]	3.940	0.588[a]	2.490	0.423[a]
Extra-AFTA trade of AFTA member countries (*AFTAEXT*)	1.470	0.471[a]	0.888	0.358[b]
Constant	−36.700	3.810[a]	−33.700	2.850[a]
R^2 (overall)	0.630		0.630	
(Within)	0.592		0.585	
(Between)	0.784		0.832	
F	9738.350		16751.340	
Number of observations	19,445		19,390	

Notes:
[1] Estimated by applying the random effect estimator to annual data on the bilateral trade of forty-one countries over the period 1992 to 2003. The standard errors (SEs) of the regression coefficients have been derived using the Huber–White consistent variance-covariance ('sandwich') estimator. The statistical significance (based on the standard t-test) is denoted as [a] (1 per cent) and [b] (5 per cent). Results for the time dummies are not reported.
[2] Other variables included in the model but deleted from the final estimate, because of their high correlation with *PGDP* (see section 4):
   TELE Main telephone lines per 1,000 people;
   ELET Per capita electricity production in kilowatts.
[3] Manufacturing wage of partner (importing) country relative to that of reporting (exporting) country, adjusted for the bilateral exchange rate.
[4] Captures membership in four regional trading agreements – AFTA, the European Union, NAFTA and Mercosur – with all countries not belonging to *any* RTA forming the base group.
[5] Including AFTA.

Table 3.6 *Definition of variables and data sources used in regression analysis*

Variable	Definition	Data source
M	Bilateral trade flows ('Component' and 'Final Goods' trade) in constant (1995) dollars	Trade flows: UN Comtrade database, online Exchange rates: IMF, *International Financial Statistics*, line rf
GDP	Real GDP (at 1995 prices)	World Bank, *World Development Indicators*
DIST	Great circle distance between the capital cities of two countries	Joe Haveman's International Trade Data, at www.macalester.edu/research/economics/PAGE/HAVEMAN/Trade.Resources/TradeData.html
RWG	Relative labour cost in manufacturing, adjusted for exchange rate changes: $$RWG_{ij} = \frac{W_i}{W_j} E_{ij}$$ where W = manufacturing wage index (1992 = 100) and E = nominal bilateral exchange rate expressed as the value of *i*'s currency in terms of *j*'s currency By construct, an increase (decrease) in RWG_{ij} indicates a deterioration (improvement) in *i*'s cost competitiveness vis-à-vis *j*	Annual manufacturing wage data for United States: US Bureau of Economic Analysis (BEA) 'Interactive database of National Income and Product Accounts Tables', at www.bea.gov/bea/dn/nipaweb/SelectTable.asp? Selected = N#S6> under Section 6 – Income and Employment by Industry All other countries: BEA online database 'Survey of US Direct Investment Abroad', at www.bea.doc.gov/bea/uguide.htm#_1_23 Bilateral exchange rates: derived from bilateral dollar exchange rates obtained from IMF, *International Financial Statistics*, line rf

in table 3.5.[12] Information on variable construction and the data sources is given in table 3.6. The countries covered in the analysis are listed in table 3.7.

In both regressions the coefficients on the two central gravity variables – the level of GDP and the distance – have the expected signs (positive and negative, respectively) and are significant at the 1 per cent level. The coefficient on GDP is similar in magnitude in the two equations, suggesting that the market size is an equally important determinant of trade in components as well as in final assembled goods. The magnitude of the

---

[12] Alternative OLS estimates are available from the authors on request. The results are remarkably resilient to the choice as to OLS and or the random effect estimator.

Table 3.7 *Country coverage*

Argentina	France	Mexico	South Africa
Australia	Germany	Netherlands	South Korea
Austria	Hong Kong SAR	Norway	Spain
Belgium	Hungary	Philippines	Sweden
Brazil	India	Poland	Switzerland
Canada	Indonesia	Portugal	Thailand
China	Ireland	Russia	Turkey
Costa Rica	Israel	Singapore	United Kingdom
Czech Republic	Italy	Slovak Republic	United States
Denmark	Japan	Slovenia	
Finland	Malaysia		

Of which, RTA member countries:

AFTA	EU 15	NAFTA	Mercosur
Indonesia	Austria	Canada	Argentina
Malaysia	Belgium/Luxembourg	United States	Brazil
Philippines	Denmark	Mexico	
Singapore	Finland		
Thailand	France		
	Germany		
	Ireland		
	Italy		
	Netherlands		
	Norway		
	Portugal		
	Spain		
	Sweden		
	United Kingdom		

coefficient on the exporter per capita GDP is remarkably similar, but markedly different from that on the importer per capita GDP, between the two equations. It seems that differences in the stage of economic development between trading partners are important only in explaining inter-country differences in component trade.

The coefficient on relative manufacturing wages (RWG) is statistically significant with the expected sign in both equations. Thus, there is strong empirical support for the hypothesis that relative wage differentials are a significant determinant of cross-border trade in parts and components (as well as the related final products). This may reflect the interconnectedness of components trade and the dependence of final exports on component imports. Interestingly, however, the magnitude of the coefficient on RWG in the component equation is much larger than that in the final goods equation. This difference suggests that the different stages of component assembly are more labour-intensive than final assembly. It is also interesting that the coefficient on | $\Delta PGDP$ | is not statistically different from zero in the component equation. This result, when interpreted in conjunction with the results for RWG, suggests that relative manufacturing wages play an important role in fragmentation-based trade regardless of differences/similarities in overall factor endowment. In other words, the Ricardian competitive advantage (as against Hecksher–Ohlin factor endowment differentials) appears to be an important factor driving cross-border trade in components (Neary, 2003).

The results for the distance variable (DST) provide strong support for the hypothesis that transportation costs and other distance-related costs are an important determinant of trade flows. Interestingly, the distance coefficient for components is larger in magnitude than that relating to final trade.[13] This difference is consistent with the hypothesis that vertical specialisation, given the multiple border crossings involved in the production process, is much more sensitive to transport cost. The common language dummy (LNG) is not statistically significant.

There is no evidence to support the hypothesis that RTAs promote fragmentation trade; the coefficients on both $RTAEXT$ and $RTAINT$ are statistically insignificant, with an unexpected (negative) sign. This result is consistent with the fact that much of the world's fragmentation trade takes place in the context of tariff concessions, overseas assembly provisions in developed countries and export promotion schemes in developing countries. Moreover, it could well be that rules of origin in RTAs deter firms involved in fragmentation-based trade from utilising the duty concessions on offer, because of the inherent difficulties in defining the 'product' for duty exemption and because of the transaction costs associated with the bureaucratic supervision of the amount of value added in production coming from various sources (Athukorala, 2005).

The coefficients on the two dummy variables for AFTA are highly significant, with a positive sign in both equations. In particular, the coefficient on $AFTAINT$ suggests that intra-AFTA component trade is about fifty times higher than the level predicted by the other explanatory variables in the model.[14] This unique result for AFTA (compared to the other RTAs) clearly points to the need for going beyond intra-regional tariff reductions (and other variables captured in our model) to understand that region's unique dynamic role in fragmentation trade. Perhaps the explanation lies in economic history: the early choice of the region

---

[13] The difference is statistically significant in both cases.

[14] Note that, as the model was estimated in logs, the percentage equivalent for any dummy coefficient is [exp (dummy coefficient) – 1] * 100.

(first Singapore and subsequently Malaysia and other countries) by MNEs as a location for outsourcing activities (Athukorala, 2005). It is well known that there is a general tendency for MNE affiliates to become increasingly embedded in host countries the longer they are present there and the more conducive the overall investment climate of the host country becomes over time. They may respond sluggishly to relative cost changes once they have invested substantial resources in domestic production facilities and in establishing information links. Moreover, site selection decisions of MNEs operating in assembly activities are strongly influenced by the presence of other key market players in the given country (Rangan and Lawrence, 1999). Finally, rapid and sustained economic expansion for over three decades in a number of countries in the region has presumably brought about a situation of 'market thickness' (the economic depth of trading nations), which positively impacts on the location of outsourcing activity.

In the previous section we noted that, compared to NAFTA and the European Union, the east Asian region is unique for the heavy concentration and rapid growth of its fragmentation trade. The results of the regression analysis enable us to come up with three explanations for this unique east Asian experience. First, the region is well placed to benefit from fragmentation-based specialisation countries in terms of relative wages. Not only are manufacturing wages in the latecomers to export-oriented industrialisation in east Asia (China, Malaysia, Thailand, Vietnam and the Philippines) low by world standards but also there are significant wage differentials between countries in the region, providing an ideal setting for the operation of cross-border production networks.[15] Second, relative cost advantages arising from these wage patterns seem to have been nicely complemented by cost/coordination advantages arising from the geographical proximity of the countries, and also perhaps the close sociocultural links between them. Third, 'first comer' advantages – 'market thickness' and 'agglomeration' benefits evolved over a long period of time – also seem to have played a key role. The latter two factors would have jointly brought about significant cost advantages in maintaining 'service links' in production networks in the region.

---

[15] The average annual compensation (salary/wage plus other remuneration) per worker in east Asian countries and selected developing countries involved in international production networks (annual average in dollars for the period 1992–2004) is as follows: China, $5,639; Indonesia, $5,356; Philippines, $6,955; Thailand, $6,474; Malaysia, $8,244; Taiwan, $22,420; South Korea, $27,350; Singapore, $22,237; Poland, $9,220; Hungary, $9,030; Czech Republic, $8,032; Mexico, $10,836; Spain, $37,578; Portugal, $20,613; and Ireland, $34,471 (source: BEA online database 'Survey of US Direct Investment Abroad', at www.bea.gov/bea/uguide.htm#_1_23).

5   Conclusions

In this chapter we have examined the extent, trends and patterns of production fragmentation in world trade using a new data set constructed by carefully separating parts and components from total trade using finely disaggregated data from the UN trade data reporting system. The major novelty of the study is the econometric analysis of the determinants of inter-country variation in the degree of dependence on this new form of international specialisation using an augmented gravity model, with special emphasis on countries in east Asia.

International production fragmentation has certainly played a pivotal role in the continuing dynamism and increasing intra-regional economic inter-dependence of the east Asian economies. This does not, however, mean that fragmentation-based international specialisation has contributed to reducing the region's dependence on the global economy. The high intra-regional trade reported in recent studies reflects rapidly expanding intra-regional trade in components. There is no evidence of rapid intra-regional trade integration in terms of final products. In fact, the region's growth dynamism based on vertical specialisation depends inescapably on its extra-regional trade in final goods, and this dependence has in fact *increased* over the years. The growing importance of China as a regional exporter and importer has begun to change the picture in recent years, but extra-regional trade is likely to remain the engine of growth for the region in the foreseeable future. Put simply, the growing trade in components has made the east Asia region increasingly reliant on extra-regional trade for its growth dynamism.

There is clear evidence that fragmentation trade is expanding more rapidly than conventional final goods trade. The degree of dependence on this new form of international specialisation is proportionately larger in east Asia than it is in North America and Europe. The results from the gravity model estimation suggest that east Asia's unique position in world fragmentation trade is based on relative labour cost advantages (both relatively low wages and, notably, variability in wages between countries), the geographical proximity of the countries and first comer advantages. The results also reveal notable differences between component trade and trade in finally assembled goods with respect to the impact of some of the key determinant trade flows. This finding makes a strong case for treating component trade separately from total trade in trade flow analysis.

References

Arndt, S. W. (1997), 'Globalization and the Open Economy', *North American Journal of Economics and Finance*, **8**, 1, 71–9.

Athukorala, P. (2005), 'Product Fragmentation and Trade Patterns in East Asia', *Asian Economic Papers*, **4**, 3, 1–27.

Baldone, S., F. Sdoagati and L. Tajoli (2001), 'Patterns and Determinants of International Fragmentation of Production: Evidence from Outward Processing Trade between the EU and Central Eastern European Countries', *Weltwirtschaftliches Archiv*, **137**, 1, 80–104.

Borrus, M. (1997), 'Left for Dead: Asian Production Networks and the Revival of US Electronics', in B. Naughton (ed.), *The China Circle: Economics and Technology in the PRC, Taiwan and Hong Kong* (Washington, DC: Brookings Institution Press), 215–39.

Brown, C., and G. Linden (2005), 'Offshoring in the Semiconductor Industry: A Historical Perspective', in S. M. Collins and L. Brainard (eds.), *Brookings Trade Forum 2005: Offshoring White-collar Work* (Washington, DC: Brooking Institution Press), 270–333.

Brown, D. K., A. V. Deardorff and R. M. Stern (2004), 'The Effect of Multinational Production on Wages and Working Conditions in Developing Countries', in R. E. Baldwin and L. A. Winters (eds.), *Challenges of Globalization: Analyzing the Economics* (Chicago: University of Chicago Press), 279–332.

Cairncross, F. (1997), *The Death of Distance: How the Communication Revolution Will Change Our Lives* (London: Orion Business Books).

Dobson, W., and S. Y. Chia (1997), *Multinationals and East Asian Integration* (Singapore: Institute of Southeast Asian Studies).

Drysdale, P., and R. Garnaut (1997), 'The Pacific: An Application of a General Theory of Economic Integration', in C. F. Bergsten and M. Noland (eds.), *Pacific Dynamism and the International Economic System* (Washington, DC: Institute for International Economics), 183–224.

Egger, H., and P. Egger (2003) 'Outsourcing and Skill-specific Employment in a Small Economy: Austria after the fall of the Iron Curtain', *Oxford Economic Papers*, **55**, 4, 625–43.

(2005), 'The Determinants of EU Processing Trade', *World Economy*, **28**, 2, 147–68.

Feenstra, R. C., R. E. Lipsey, H. Deng, A. C. Ma and H. Mo (2005), 'World Trade Flows, 1962–2000', Working Paper no. 11040, National Bureau of Economic Research, Cambridge, MA.

Frankel, J. A., and S. Wei (1997), 'The New Regionalism and Asia: Impact and Policy Options', in A. Panagariya, M. G. Quibria and N. Rao (eds.), *The Global Trading System and Developing Asia* (Oxford: Oxford University Press), 83–130.

Görg, H. (2000), 'Fragmentation and Trade: US Inward Processing Trade in the EU', *Weltwirtschaftliches Archiv*, **136**, 3, 403–22.

Grossman, G. M., and E. Helpman (2005), 'Outsourcing in a Global Economy', *Review of Economic Studies*, **72**, 1, 135–59.

Helleiner, G. K. (1973), 'Manufactured Exports from Less Developed Countries and Multinational Firms', *Economic Journal*, **83**, March, 21–47.

Helpman, E. (1987), 'Imperfect Competition and International Trade: Evidence from Fourteen Industrial Countries', *Journal of the Japanese and International Economies*, **1**, 1, 62–81.

Hummels, D. (2001), 'Have International Transport Costs Declined?', *Journal of International Economics*, **54**, 1, 75–96

Jones, R. W. (2000), *Globalization and the Theory of Input Trade* (Cambridge, MA: MIT Press).

Jones, R. W., and H. Kierzkowski (1990), 'The Role of Services in Production and International Trade: A Theoretical Framework', in R. W. Jones and A. O. Krueger (eds.), *The Political Economy of International Trade: Essays in Honor of Robert Baldwin* (Oxford: Basil Blackwell), 31–48.

(2001), 'Globalization and the Consequences of International Fragmentation', in R. Dornbusch, G. Calvo and M. Obstfeld (eds.), *Money, Factor Mobility and Trade: The Festschrift in Honor of Robert A. Mundell* (Cambridge, MA: MIT Press), 365–81.

Jones, R. W., H. Kierzkowski and C. Lurong (2004), 'What Does the Evidence Tell Us about Fragmentation and Outsourcing?', *International Review of Economics and Finance*, **14**, 3, 305–16.

Kierzkowski, H. (2001), 'Joining the Global Economy: Experience and Prospects of the Transition Economies', in S. W. Arndt and H. Kierzkowski (eds.), *Fragmentation: New Production Patterns in the World Economy* (Oxford: Oxford University Press), 231–53.

Kwan, C. H. (2001), *Yen Bloc: Toward Economic Integration in Asia* (Washington, DC: Brookings Institution Press).

McKendrick, D. G., R. F. Doner and S. Haggard (2000), *From Silicon Valley to Singapore: Location and Competitive Advantage in the Hard Disk Drive Industry* (Stanford, CA: Stanford University Press).

Neary, P. (2003), 'Competitive versus Comparative Advantage', *World Economy*, **26**, 4, 457–70.

Ng, F., and A. Yeats (2001), 'Production Sharing in East Asia: Who Does What for Whom, and Why?', in L. K. Cheng and H. Kierzkowski (eds.), *Global Production and Trade in East Asia* (Boston: Kluwer Academic), 63–109.

(2003), 'Major Trade Trends in East Asia: What Are Their Implications for Regional Cooperation and Growth?', Policy Research Working Paper no. 3084, World Bank, Washington, DC.

Petri, P. (1993), 'The East Asian Trading Block: An Analytical History', in J. A. Frankel and M. Kahler (eds.), *Regionalism and Rivalry: Japan and the United State in Pacific Asia* (Chicago: Chicago University Press), 21–48.

Rangan, S., and R. Lawrence (1999), *A Prism on Globalization* (Washington, DC: Brookings Institution Press).

Sturgeon, T. J. (2003), 'What Really Goes on in Silicon Valley? Spatial Clustering and Dispersal in Modular Production Networks', *Journal of Economic Geography*, **3**, 2, 199–225.

Venables, A. J. (1999), 'Fragmentation and Multinational Production', *European Economic Review*, **43**, 3, 935–45.

Wooldridge, J. (2001), *Econometric Analysis of Cross-section and Panel Data* (Cambridge, MA: MIT Press).

Yi, K. (2003), 'Can Vertical Specialization Explain the Growth of World Trade?', *Journal of Political Economy*, **111**, 1, 52–102.

4 Going global: trade, internationalisation of production and domestic performance of euro area firms

Ingo Geishecker, Holger Görg and Daria Taglioni[1]

1 Introduction

Recent empirical research highlights the fact that firms show a large degree of heterogeneity in their productivity, size, export intensity and propensity to invest and produce abroad and react differently to the increased trade openness and to the broader structural changes associated with increased regional and worldwide economic integration. International trade models that specifically address firm heterogeneity bring to the fore a number of previously unexplored channels through which the international activity of firms, through exporting (which has received most attention) or outward FDI, is linked to a country's productivity and, therefore, to its competitiveness on international markets (e.g. Melitz, 2003, Bernard *et al.*, 2003, and Helpman *et al.*, 2004).

In a nutshell, the most widely cited predictions and testable hypotheses of the models accounting for firm heterogeneity are twofold. First, firms that serve foreign markets are assumed to be more productive than their purely domestic competitors. The extension by Helpman *et al.* (2004) also predicts that firms investing abroad are the most productive, followed by exporters and purely domestic firms. Second, once countries open up to trade this modifies the set of firms that trade and invest abroad as well as the range of destinations covered and the set of goods traded (the so-called 'extensive margin of trade'), leading to important effects on international trade flows via changes in aggregate productivity through the reallocation of factors of production among different types of firms. Specifically, one would expect the least productive firms to exit and their market share to be covered by more productive firms, thus raising aggregate industry-level productivity. One would also expect that a country

---

[1] Respectively University of Göttingen; Leverhulme Centre for Research on Globalisation and Economic Policy, University of Nottingham; and External Developments Division, European Central Bank, Frankfurt.

whose share of exporting and multinational enterprises increases over time will experience an increase in aggregate productivity as well as in aggregate competitiveness on international markets (Ottaviano *et al.*, 2007).

Confirmed by the data, these predictions help to solve puzzles about the effects of globalisation that neither neoclassical nor new trade theories are able to account for. For one, they offer an explanation as to why firms with very different size and productivity levels survive and coexist in the same sector and in the same market, before and after an increase in trade openness or moves towards global and regional integration. More importantly, they also make clear why exposure to trade (be it with regional trade partners or global in scope) seems to oblige some firms to shut down and some products and varieties to be discontinued while at the same time increasing average aggregate productivity, even without a change in other determinants of firm performance, and foremost in technology.

Much of the existing empirical research has focused on the first prediction, namely the question whether exporters, and MNEs, are more productive than purely domestic firms.[2] While many of the studies measuring productivity divergence among types of firms focused on performance differences between exporters and non-exporters, a smaller literature has emerged extending this type of analysis to investigating productivity differences between MNEs, exporters and purely domestic firms. The theoretical model by Helpman *et al.* (2004) suggests a productivity ranking that would show MNEs to be the most productive, followed by exporters and then non-exporters. Head and Ries (2003), using Japanese data, fail to find evidence in favour of such a ranking, but further studies by, for example, Girma *et al.* (2004) for Ireland, Castellani and Zanfei (2004) for Italy, Arnold and Hussinger (2005) for Germany, and Girma *et al.* (2005) for the United Kingdom show that MNEs are the most productive among the three types of firms. Ironically, however, the studies for Ireland and Italy are less successful in establishing that non-multinational exporters are also more productive than purely domestic firms (once the fact that many exporters are also multinationals has been accounted for), while the studies for Germany and the United

---

[2] In terms of showing performance premia for exporters versus non-exporters, early studies such as Clerides *et al.* (1998) for Colombia, Mexico and Morocco and Bernard and Jensen (1999) for the United States find convincing evidence that new exporters are, on average, more productive than non-exporters. Since then, these results have been replicated for a large number of countries, as recently comprehensively reviewed by Wagner (2005) and Greenaway and Kneller (2008). As concerns euro area countries, evidence is available for Germany, France, Italy and Spain (e.g. Bernard and Wagner, 2001, Eaton *et al.*, 2003, Castellani, 2002, Delgado *et al.*, 2002, and Wagner, 2005).

Kingdom provide full support for the productivity ranking as predicted by the model.

This chapter relates to and extends this recent literature on differences between different firm types in terms of their international engagement. To the best knowledge of the authors, this is the first study that looks at these issues using firm-level data related to the whole euro area. We concern ourselves with the question of whether exporters, and MNEs, are more productive than purely domestic firms and whether firms with different levels of productivity have different internationalisation strategies. We present evidence based on firms from the twelve euro area countries and compare it with evidence from the United Kingdom utilising a large firm-level panel data set, Amadeus, for 2004. We report on aspects of heterogeneity in the data and, as far as possible, compare them with findings from other countries. Furthermore, we quantify the performance premium of being an exporter or a multinational, in line with previous literature for other countries. Most importantly, for the best-performing group of firms – firms with affiliates abroad (i.e. MNEs) – we uncover meaningful correlations between their internationalisation strategies in terms of the magnitude of their foreign engagement (and the regional versus global location of their operations) and the underlying characteristics of the parent firm, such as size, profits and productivity.

The remainder of the chapter is structured as follows. Section 2 describes our data set, assesses how representative it is of firm activity in the euro area and presents some first insight into aspects of firm-level heterogeneity in the data. Section 3 investigates patterns of exporting and multinational activity in the data, and assesses whether there are performance differences along a number of firm characteristics between these different types of firms. Section 4 looks in more detail at MNEs in the data, charting the magnitude and location of their operations and the relationship between these aspects of multinational activity and firm performance. Section 5 then goes on to describe patterns of entry and exit into multinationality in the euro area. Finally, Section 6 summarises and concludes.

2   Description of the data

This chapter uses a cross-section of about 250,000 manufacturing firms from the twelve euro area countries and from the United Kingdom relating to the fiscal year 2004. The data are from the Amadeus database (Bureau van Dijk, BvD), which provides comparable firm-level balance sheet data for 4 million companies in thirty-four European countries in four-digit NACE[3] sectoral detail and covers all industries, with the exception of the bank and insurance sectors. Amadeus gathers information on firms that satisfy country-specific size thresholds. By construction, the database is biased towards large companies. A further shortcoming of the data is that statutory reporting and filing requirements differ from country to country, and the amount of balance sheet information required by each country varies correspondingly, with the result that the data coverage is very unbalanced. In addition, Amadeus is less complete, to date, in countries where there is a lack of centralisation, with companies registering at offices based in their region rather than at a single registry. This is a problem in particular for Germany, where, furthermore, value added data is available only for a small subset of companies.

2.1   Representativeness of the sample

Table 4.1 shows the coverage in terms of value added and employment for each country obtained by comparing our sample with aggregate data for manufacturing taken from the sixty-industry database of the Groningen Growth and Development Centre (GGDC). Although some observations are missing for particular indicators and countries, our final sample is fairly representative of the overall economies in selected countries. Average employment and value added coverage are, respectively, around 44 per cent and 40 per cent, with peaks well above 60 per cent for the figures relating to Belgium, Finland, France and Spain.

Tables 4.2 and 4.3 summarise the number of firms, employment and value added distribution of our final sample broken down by size class, and broad sector. As expected, compared to the data set we use as a benchmark, the OECD Business by Size Class (BSC) data set, our sample systematically under-represents firms with fewer than fifty employees. Table 4.2 shows that the bias towards large firms is important both in the euro area and in the United Kingdom. Furthermore, table 4.3 indicates that sectors in which production tends to be concentrated among a relatively small number of firms (e.g. chemicals, rubber and plastics, transport equipment) tend to be over-represented, due to their constituency of firms that are larger on average. By contrast, sectors with fairly dispersed production (as in printing and publishing industries, textiles and machinery) seem to be most under-represented in terms of both employment and value added generated. For the euro area as an

---

[3] NACE is the European Union's industrial classification system.

Table 4.1 *Representativeness of the Amadeus sample*

	Number of firms in Amadeus data set	Amadeus as share of GGDC sixty-industry database	
		Employment (number engaged)	Value added (€ thousands)
Euro area	236,289	44%	40%
of which:			
Austria	4,071	38%	22%
Belgium	6,382	75%	92%
Finland	8,218	71%	64%
France	80,622	85%	83%
Germany	27,752	30%	16%
Greece	6,005	48%	n.a.
Ireland	409	15%	n.a.
Italy	31,095	35%	44%
Luxembourg	1	0%	n.a.
Netherlands	794	11%	15%
Portugal	477	7%	13%
Spain	70,463	61%	64%
United Kingdom	10,077	51%	60%

Table 4.2 *Representativeness of the Amadeus sample by size of employment (share of each size class as a percentage of the total)*

	Amadeus			OECD BSC		
	Firms	Employees	Turnover	Firms	Employees	Turnover
Percentage of small firms (fewer than 50 employees)						
Euro area	86	23	15	96	33	21
United Kingdom	44	4	6	93	28	18
Percentage of medium-sized firms (from 50 to 249 employees)						
Euro area	11	26	21	4	25	21
United Kingdom	41	25	20	6	27	22
Percentage of large firms (250 or more employees)						
Euro area	3	51	64	1	43	59
United Kingdom	15	71	74	1	45	61

aggregate, the weight of these sectors in manufacturing is on average between two and three percentage points smaller according to the data from Amadeus than what is reported in the GGDC sixty-industry database.

Table 4.3 *Representativeness of the Amadeus euro area sample, by sector*

Industries	NACE codes	Firms	Share of each sector as percentage of total manufacturing in Amadeus		Share of each sector as percentage of total manufacturing in GGDC sixty-industry database		Difference between sectoral shares in Amadeus and GGDC sixty-industry database	
			Employment (number of employees)	Value added	Employment (number engaged)	Value added	Employment	Value added
Food, drinks and tobacco	15–16	31,172	10%	10%	13%	12%	–3%	–2%
Textiles, clothing, leather and footwear	17–19	18,967	6%	4%	9%	6%	–4%	–2%
Wood, paper and publishing	20–22	37,113	9%	8%	11%	11%	–2%	–3%
Chemical, rubber and plastics	24–25	16,418	13%	17%	10%	15%	3%	1%
Metals	23, 26–28	56,848	19%	21%	20%	19%	–1%	2%
Machinery	29–30	22,127	11%	10%	11%	12%	0%	–2%
Electrical, communication and optical equipment	31–33	17,433	9%	9%	10%	11%	–1%	–2%
Transport equipment	34–35	6,171	11%	12%	9%	11%	2%	1%
Total manufacturing	D	236,289	100%	100%	100%	100%	100%	100%

2.2   Firm heterogeneity in the sample

Heterogeneity is a strong feature of our data, holding true for a variety of performance measures and, importantly, cutting across industries. While inter-industry differences certainly matter for choices about trade and FDI, firm-level heterogeneity suggests that trade and FDI orientation seems to have less to do with industry per se than standard trade models might suggest. Firms within narrowly defined sectors are, comparatively, as diverse and dispersed as firms from the overall distribution when measured in terms of their productivity (measured as value added per worker), profits, turnover and employment.

As table 4.4 indicates, in the euro area, manufacturing firms one standard deviation away from the median firm are 7 per cent more labour-productive, 57 per cent more profitable, sell 26 per cent more and employ 63 per cent more of the workforce. Such dispersion is barely lower within narrowly defined NACE four-digit sectors:[4] firms one standard deviation away from the intra-industry median firm are 6 per cent more labour-productive, 51 per cent more profitable, have 24 per cent higher turnover and employ 59 per cent more workers. Similar results hold true for dispersion among UK firms. Moreover, the same trends emerge if we measure dispersion from the average instead of the median.

Our findings match measures of overall and intra-industry dispersion reported by other studies and measured on alternative data sets. Bernard *et al.* (2003) find that the standard deviation of log productivity within 458 four-digit manufacturing sectors in the United States has a value of 0.66, while the unconditional standard deviation is only slightly higher, at a value of 0.75. This indicates a high level of heterogeneity in their data set. Furthermore, they find that these results hold true also for other key measures of firm performance, including capital intensity (measured as total assets per worker) and skill intensity (measured as the share of non-production workers over labour costs).

One could argue that static heterogeneity matters little for aggregate cross-sector effects and that, despite the observed intra-firm heterogeneity, firms in a sector, while being different from each other, tend to move in the same direction over time and in response to the business cycle, so that it is still possible to speak of an 'average response' to given exogenous shocks or to business cycle developments by firms belonging to the same sector. Nonetheless, Davis and Haltiwanger (1992) and Davis *et al.* (1996), using plant-level longitudinal evidence on job flows in the United States and controlling for different sensitivities of sectors to the

---

[4] There are 241 NACE four-digit sectors.

Table 4.4 *Heterogeneity of manufacturing firms (percentages)*

Euro area

	How much bigger are firms one standard deviation from median firm?				How much bigger are firms one standard deviation from average firm?			
	Turnover	Employment	Productivity	Profits	Turnover	Employment	Productivity	Profits
All industries	126.4	162.7	106.6	156.7	125.7	160.9	106.6	154.5
within two-digit NACE industries	125.3	161.4	106.4	154.3	124.7	159.1	106.4	152.7
within four-digit NACE industries	123.7	158.8	106.2	151.5	123.3	157.1	106.2	150.6

United Kingdom

	How much bigger are firms one standard deviation from median firm?				How much bigger are firms one standard deviation from average firm?			
	Turnover	Employment	Productivity	Profits	Turnover	Employment	Productivity	Profits
All industries	122.9	140.6	106.4	134.5	123.6	142.7	106.4	135.0
within two-digit NACE industries	126.1	163.2	106.4	153.9	125.5	160.2	106.4	152.2
within four-digit NACE industries	125.4	160.4	106.3	150.6	125.0	158.0	106.3	149.7

business cycle, find that sectoral shock theories leading to firms' shifts out of one sector and into another sector cannot account for much of the observed magnitude or variation in job reallocation in their data. They show that 'between-sector shifts' are able to explain only between 5 and 10 per cent of ongoing job creation and job destruction. The remaining 90 to 95 per cent of employment change, though, cannot be explained by theories that stress learning about initial conditions but nor does it represent 'white noise', as it exhibits highly significant persistence over time and statistically robust correlation with aggregate employment dynamics.

In summary, evidence from the data set exploited in the current study and from other empirical studies shows that it is difficult to speak about an average sectoral response to shocks and changes in the external environment, since firms within industries – as narrowly defined as the data allow – exhibit substantial heterogeneity along a number of important firm-level characteristics as well as in their behaviour vis-à-vis business cycle changes.

3   Exports and multinational activity

We also find in our data that, within the same industry, some firms export while many others do not, and that an even smaller subset owns production facilities abroad/has a multinational status.[5] Within our data set, it is only with France and the United Kingdom that we can jointly analyse exporting behaviour and foreign investment by firms. Hence, in order to establish the link between export and foreign investment behaviour we focus on data from these countries.

As table 4.5 shows, in 2004 40 per cent of all UK manufacturing firms sampled in Amadeus exported.[6] In France, exporters accounted for an even lower share, with only 35 per cent of all French manufacturing firms being exporters and 64 per cent having fully domestic operations.[7] Such a concentration of export activity among a relatively small number of firms is mirrored in other studies. For example, using a data set on French firms generated by merging customs and tax administration data, Eaton *et al.*

---

[5] This constitutes a challenge from the data to standard trade theories. According to new trade theory, for instance, a country's move from autarchy to trade should induce all domestic firms to export a portion of their production. With every increase in freeness of trade, each firm should increase the volume of its exports in line with the reduced cost of exporting the merchandise. This 'challenge' has been addressed in the recent heterogeneous firm models, such as Bernard *et al.* (2003), Melitz (2003) and Montagna (2001).

[6] This figure excludes MNEs that also export. With this group of firms the share of UK firms that exported in 2004 rises to 43 per cent.

[7] In France, the share of exporters rises to 36 per cent if we include MNEs that also export.

Table 4.5 *Contributions of different types of firms to domestic employment, turnover and value added (per cent)*

Percentage of total manufacturing	Domestic firms	Exporters (excluding MNEs that also export)	All MNEs
		Euro area	
Number of firms	97	–	3
Employment	71	–	29
Turnover	60	–	40
Value added	57	–	43
		France	
Number of firms	64	34	2
Employment	24	50	26
Turnover	15	43	42
Value added	15	48	37
		United Kingdom	
Number of firms	54	40	5
Employment	42	46	12
Turnover	37	46	17
Value added	36	46	18

Note: – = data not available.

(2004) find that as little as 17.4 per cent of firms exported in 1986.[8] Aggregate French exports as a share of GDP increased by almost twelve percentage points over the period 1986–2004. Hence, the difference between the number of French exporters in our study and in the study by Eaton *et al.* simply mirrors this evolution, and, furthermore, it indicates that the increase in French exports over the last twenty years was mostly driven by new firms entering the export business rather than by pre-existing exporters selling increasing volumes of their products abroad, in line with predictions of models of trade with firm heterogeneity.

While previous studies have looked only at exports, our data set allows us also to consider firms with foreign affiliates abroad – i.e. MNEs. The data in table 4.5 indicate that fewer than 2 per cent of French manufacturing firms and little more than 5 per cent of British manufacturing firms have affiliates abroad. Nevertheless, these firms account, in France, for 26 per cent of total manufacturing employment, 42 per cent of turnover and 37 per cent of value added and, in the United Kingdom, for 12 per cent of

---

[8] Eaton *et al.* (200) also report a comparable figure for the United States (taken from Bernard and Jensen, 1999) in 1985, where 14.6 per cent of firms export. Furthermore, Bernard and Wagner (2001) show that around 44 per cent of firms in their sample of firms in Lower Saxony (Germany) exported in 1986.

total manufacturing employment, 17 per cent of turnover and 18 per cent of value added. In other words, it is, on average, large firms that contribute high levels of economic activity to these countries.

Firms that have operations in more than one foreign country account, roughly, for only 1 per cent of the total number of euro area manufacturing firms in our data set, though they account for an over-proportional share of economic activity, generating 20 per cent of employment, 30 per cent of turnover and 33 per cent of value added in the sample.

Another interesting aspect borne out by the data is that not only is the subset of firms with international engagement (i.e. exporters or foreign affiliates) very small, but also activity within the exporter and multinational groups of firms is very highly concentrated, with very few firms covering most of the export and multinational activity. In France, the largest 1 per cent traders generate 61 per cent of total export turnover – a finding similar to that of Bernard et al. (2005), who also show that export activity is highly concentrated. Furthermore, our data for France show that the top 1 per cent of MNEs employ 43 per cent of total multinational labour in the home country, and generate 66 per cent of the overall multinational turnover and 58 per cent of the overall multinational value added in the country. These figures are, again, similar for the United Kingdom, where the largest 1 per cent of exporters generate 40 per cent of overall turnover, and the largest 1 per cent of MNEs generate 25 per cent, 38 per cent and 40 per cent of overall multinational employment, turnover and value added, respectively. Similarly, in the euro area, the largest 1 per cent of MNEs account for 38 per cent of employment by MNEs and 57 per cent of both turnover and value added generated by MNEs, respectively.

While the evidence above shows heterogeneity in productivity, export and multinational activity, figure 4.1 brings out the striking association between the three. The figures, which use data for France and the United Kingdom, separately, and plot the kernel density distributions of various size (turnover, employment and profits) and labour productivity measures, show that exporters with no foreign affiliates are larger in size and profits, and are more productive than purely domestic firms that have no exports and no foreign affiliates. This is in line with a large literature showing the premia to exporting in a number of firm characteristics (e.g. Bernard and Jensen, 1999, Castellani, 2002, and Arnold and Hussinger, 2005). In addition, the figures show that multinational firms that have affiliates abroad are also larger and more productive than firms that serve only domestic markets or that only export. Again, this corroborates the findings of a much smaller literature investigating the differences between MNEs, exporters and purely domestic firms (e.g. Helpman et al., 2004, and Girma et al., 2004).

France

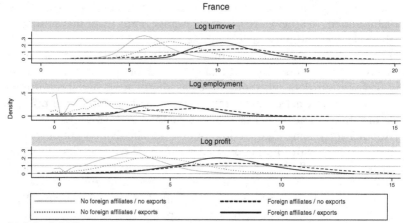

Source: Amadeus, authors' calculations.

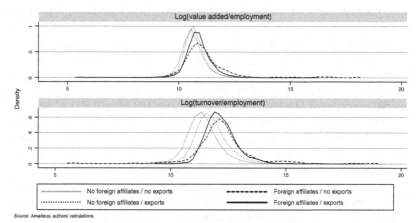

Source: Amadeus, authors' calculations.

Kolmogorov–Smirnov test – H0: the cumulative distribution of MNEs with many affiliates stochastically dominates that of MNEs with only one affiliate (3), which in turn dominates that of exporters (2), which in turn dominates that of domestic firms with domestic affiliates or no affiliates (1)

	(1)	(2)	(3)
Log turnover	1.00	0.92	0.00
Log employment	1.00	1.00	0.00
Log profit	1.00	1.00	0.00
Log(turnover/employment)	1.00	0.77	0.31
Log(value added/employment)	0.99	1.00	0.00

Figure 4.1 Domestic firms versus exporters and exporters versus MNEs (France and the United Kingdom, various size and performance measures)

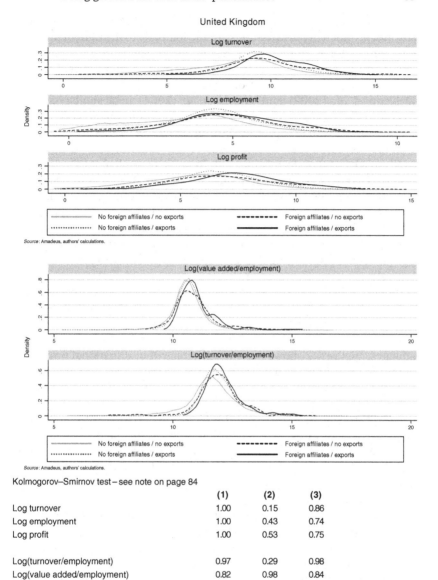

Figure 4.1 *(cont.)*

Our conclusions are based on the fact that the MNEs' and exporters' size and productivity distributions are substantially to the right of the same distribution for purely domestic firms, hence suggesting that they are larger and more productive. In order to provide a more formal test we can invoke the concept of first-order stochastic dominance, as applied by Delgado *et al.* (2002) and Girma *et al.* (2004) in a similar context. Accordingly, if we have two cumulative distribution functions (F and G) for two comparison groups, say, the productivity of MNEs and exporters, then the first-order stochastic dominance of F with respect to G is defined as $F(z) - G(z) \leq 0$ uniformly in $z \in \Re$. In order to implement the comparison we adopt the non-parametric one-sided Kolmogorov–Smirnov (KS) test, in a manner similar to Delgado *et al.* (2002) and Girma *et al.* (2004).[9] This one-sided test essentially checks the hypothesis that F stochastically dominates G; i.e. that $F(z) - G(z) \leq 0$. In order to conclude that this is the case we want to be unable to reject the null hypothesis for this one-sided test. The figures also report the p-values obtained from the tests. As can be seen, we are unable to reject the null in all cases – i.e. the cumulative distributions of MNEs with many affiliates stochastically dominates that of MNEs with only one affiliate, which in turn dominates that of exporters, which in turn dominates that of domestic firms with domestic affiliates, which in turn dominates that of domestic firms with no affiliates. Figure 4.2 shows that the advantage of multinational firms over domestic firms holds also over the sample for the whole euro area.

Table 4.6 quantifies the advantage of being an MNE in the euro area. Similar differences hold for other variables, including employment, turnover and profits. In France and the United Kingdom, exporters have a slight advantage in average labour productivity in manufacturing over purely domestic firms, while firms with foreign affiliates (either with or without exporting) are more productive still. Interestingly, MNEs that also export are slightly less productive, and smaller, than firms with foreign affiliates that do not.

In conclusion, for understanding otherwise puzzling aspects of the relationship between trade, international production sharing and firm characteristics, we have to look at new dimensions, namely at the extent to which domestic firms serve foreign markets and use foreign facilities to enhance their productivity and survive in increasingly competitive markets. To this end, and in order to provide some comparative perspective with data for the overall euro area, we now turn to focusing in more detail on MNEs, and the number and location of their foreign affiliates.

---

[9] Further details on this procedure can be found in these two papers.

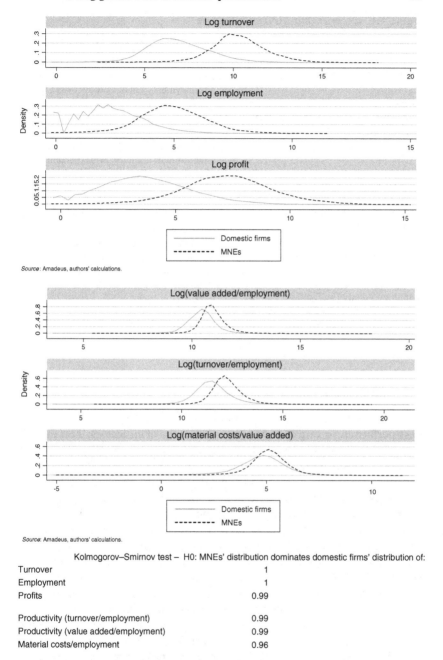

Figure 4.2 Domestic firms versus MNEs (euro area, various size and performance measures)

Table 4.6 *Exporter and MNE advantages*

	Euro area		
	Advantage of multi-establishment domestic firms over single-establishment domestic firms (percentages)		
	Turnover	Employment	Labour productivity	Profits
All industries	33	76	4	66
Within two-digit NACE industries	32	75	3	64
Within four-digit NACE industries	30	74	3	60
	Advantage of multi-establishment MNEs over single-establishment domestic firms (percentages)		
	Turnover	Employment	Labour productivity	Profits
All industries	60	145	7	126
Within two-digit NACE industries	58	141	6	123
Within four-digit NACE industries	57	143	6	120
	Advantage of MNEs with one foreign affiliate over domestic firms – single- and multi-establishment (percentages)		
	Turnover	Employment	Labour productivity	Profits
All industries	43	99	4	80
Within two-digit NACE industries	42	99	4	79
Within four-digit NACE industries	41	102	4	78

Note: Advantage is measured as the difference between two subsamples (log-normalised measure, in per cent).

4   Location choices of MNEs

From the analysis above, multinational enterprises clearly emerge as the best-performing group of firms over a wide range of indicators. This may be because of two not necessarily mutually exclusive reasons. First, the recent heterogeneous firm model by Helpman *et al.* (2004) investigates the choice between exporting and FDI and suggests that only the most efficient and productive firms will choose to do the latter. This is essentially a consequence of fixed costs, which are assumed to be higher for FDI than for exporting. Hence, firms have to have a threshold level of efficiency in order to overcome these fixed costs, and only the most efficient will be able to do so. A second possibility is that firms' use of foreign facilities enhances their productivity as they can fragment their production activities, which allows them to leverage on comparative advantages of more than one location and, in so doing, be more resilient to business cycle developments.

Once we focus on the best-performing group of firms (i.e. the MNEs) in the euro area we can investigate the trends in foreign direct investment. Within the group of MNEs, as one may perhaps expect, firms that are on average the best performers in terms of productivity, profits and turnover have a higher

Table 4.7 *Average number of foreign affiliates (overall, per location and per MNE)*

	Average number of foreign affiliates		
Overall	27.0		
By group of firms according to performance criteria:	Worst-performing firms	Middle-performance firms	Best-performing firms
Turnover	7.0	17.6	56.5
Profits	11.2	10.4	61.5
Labour productivity	9.0	13.0	57.9
	Average number of foreign affiliates per location		
Overall	2.8		
By group of firms according to performance criteria:	Worst-performing firms	Middle-performance firms	Best-performing firms
Turnover	1.6	2.4	4.5
Profits	1.7	2.0	4.8
Labour productivity	1.9	1.9	4.7
	Average number of locations per MNE		
Overall	2.5		
By group of firms according to performance criteria:	Worst-performing firms	Middle-performance firms	Best-performing firms
Turnover	1.7	3.0	5.4
Profits	1.9	2.5	5.9
Labour productivity	2.1	2.7	4.2

number of foreign affiliates, with the best-performing MNEs having on average over fifty-five affiliates, while those MNEs at the bottom end of the distribution have only between seven and eleven affiliates. Moreover, we also find that the best performers have, on average, two to four times more affiliates per location than the other two classes of firms. Finally, we also find that firms that are on average the best performers establish foreign affiliates in a larger number of locations than relatively poor performers. The contrast here is even starker when looking at the number of firms per location: this latter type of firm (defined as the bottom third in terms of the respective firm characteristics) on average establishes affiliates in two locations, whereas the top third of the firms in the sample goes to four to six locations, depending on the firm characteristic used to rank firms.

Figures 4.3(a) and 4.3(b) depict charts similar to those presented in figures 4.1 and 4.2 and described in section 3, but now compare the distribution of turnover, employment, profits and labour productivity for three types of MNE: those with only one foreign affiliate, those with between two and four, and those with more than four, respectively. As can

Number of foreign affiliates (size measures)

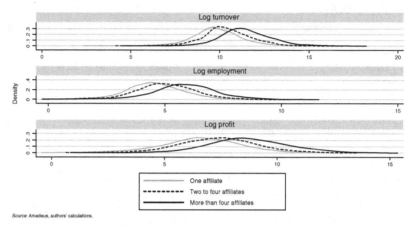

Source: Amadeus, authors' calculations.

Number of foreign affiliates (success measures)

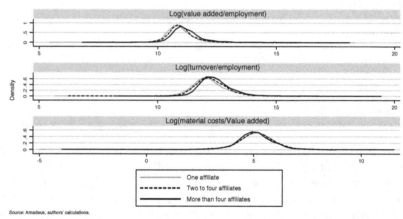

Source: Amadeus, authors' calculations.

Kolmogorov–Smirnov test per number of foreign affiliates	Turnover	Employment	Profits	Labour productivity (va/empl)	Labour productivity (turnover/ empl)	Material costs/va
More than one affiliate versus one affiliate	0.99	0.99	0.99	0.99	0.94	0.68
More than four affiliates versus two to four	0.99	0.99	0.99	0.99	1	0.01

Figure 4.3 Size and performance differences of firms
(a) Size and performance differences of firms with different numbers of
foreign affiliates

Geographical spread (size measures)

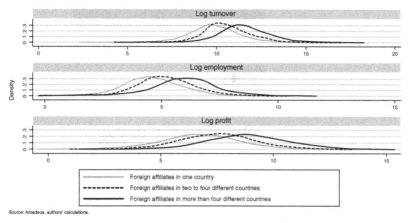

Source: Amadeus, authors' calculations.

Geographical spread (success measures)

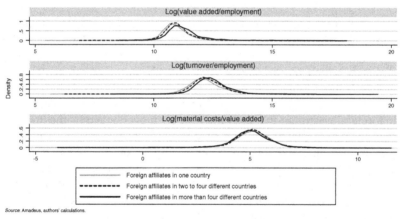

Source: Amadeus, authors' calculations.

Kolmogorov–Smirnov test per number of foreign affiliates	Turnover	Employment	Profits	Labour productivity (va/empl)	Labour productivity (turnover/empl)	Material costs/va
More than one foreign location versus one	0.99	0.99	0.99	0.99	0.79	0.04
More than four foreign locations versus two	0.99	0.96	0.99	0.99	0.99	0.04

Figure 4.3 (b) Size and performance differences of firms with different geographical spread

92   *I. Geishecker, H. Görg and D. Taglioni*

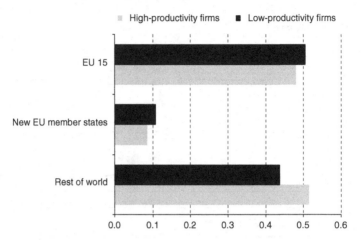

Figure 4.4 Domestic MNEs' share of affiliates in different world regions, by firms' productivity level

be seen from the KS test statistics provided at the bottom of the figure, the cumulative distribution for those with many foreign affiliates for all firm characteristics stochastically dominates that of firms with two to four affiliates, which in turn again stochastically dominates that of MNEs with only one foreign affiliate.

The analysis thus far suggests an important aspect of heterogeneity in foreign investment that has until now been overlooked by the literature: that there is a strong ranking of MNEs according to the number of foreign affiliates, and this holds for a number of size and performance characteristics. To explore this aspect of heterogeneity among euro area MNEs further, we show in figure 4.4 that larger shares of affiliates by low-productivity firms opt for locations within Europe. Some 50 per cent of affiliates of low-productivity euro area firms are located in a country of the fifteen old EU member states, while this location is chosen by only 48 per cent of affiliates of high-productivity euro area firms. Similarly, while 11 per cent of low-productivity firms go to one of the twelve new EU member states, only 9 per cent of the high-productivity firms' affiliates locate there. The situation is reversed for the rest of the world, which is the preferred location for 51 per cent of the high-productivity firms' affiliates but only 44 per cent of the low-productivity firms' affiliates. In absolute numbers, however, highly productive MNEs are present in each of these world regions with a higher number of foreign affiliates.

Foreign affiliates are also quite concentrated geographically. We show in figure 4.5 that the three top destinations for euro area MNEs (France,

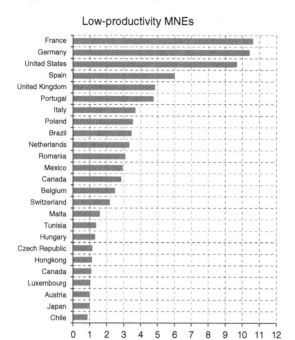

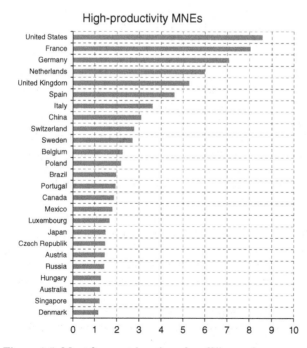

Figure 4.5 Most frequent locations for affiliates of euro area MNEs

Germany and the United States) host over a quarter of all foreign affiliates, and as few as eight countries receive over 50 per cent of all euro area foreign affiliates. While, overall, the most popular destinations for euro area firms are France and Germany, once we focus on firms with high productivity the most popular destination is the United States. Assuming that, on account of geographic proximity and perhaps other factors, including the assumption that sunk costs for setting up affiliates in other euro area countries are less than those for setting up affiliates outside the euro area, this finding is in line with reasoning from an intuitive extension of the Helpman *et al.* (2004) model discussed above. Due to higher sunk costs, only the most productive firms will choose to go predominantly to the United States, and our simple analysis is in line with this suggestion.

It is also interesting to note that, among the most frequent locations shown in the graphs, there are only three industrialising countries outside the European Union, namely China, Mexico and Brazil, that could be seen as locations for firms attempting to relocate production to low-cost countries. By far the largest share of foreign affiliates are set up in other high-income developed countries, suggesting that market access is an important motive for investing abroad by euro area firms.

Given that investment by euro area firms in low-cost countries is an important topic of political and popular debate, not least because of the feared job losses associated with such investment, we now investigate this phenomenon a little further. First we establish whether there is an observable difference in the share of affiliates in low-cost countries across the best-, medium- and poor-performing MNEs. This is depicted in figure 4.6. Here we find that, for example, MNEs in the bottom third of the turnover distribution have roughly 40 per cent of their affiliates in low-cost countries, while the top performers have only 36 per cent of their affiliates in these countries. Hence, top performers have a higher average share of affiliates in industrialised countries, which is in line with the finding depicted in figure 4.4 and accords well with the reasoning that investing in industrialised countries involves higher sunk costs. Of course, an alternative explanation is that poor-performing MNEs are forced to locate in low-income countries in order to boost their performance by lowering the operating costs of their foreign operations.

Whether such a strategy may be reasonable can be investigated by looking at the performance difference between firms that invest in such a location and those that do not. Specifically, do MNEs that establish foreign affiliates in low-cost countries have a better performance than firms that do not? Figure 4.6 presents, similarly to the analysis above, charts of the density distribution of firm characteristics, distinguishing

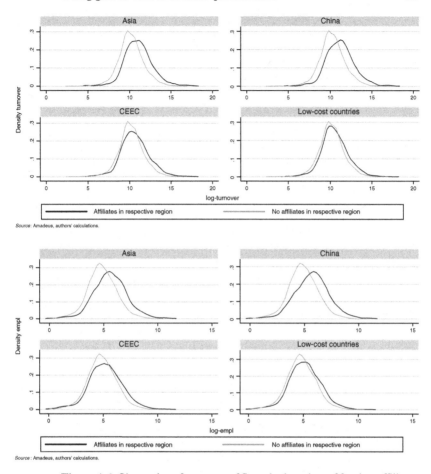

Figure 4.6 Size and performance of firms by location of foreign affiliates

between those firms that invest in a given location and those that do not. We also report the associated KS tests of first-order statistical dominance. According to the data, firms that locate in Asia and, in particular, China have a superior performance over those that do not invest there. This holds for a number of size and performance characteristics (turnover, employment, profits, productivity). This analysis is, to the best of our knowledge, the first to document such patterns, which suggests that further research into these location patterns, and the associated relationship to firm characteristics, may be very fruitful and should be able to provide important conclusions for policy-makers.

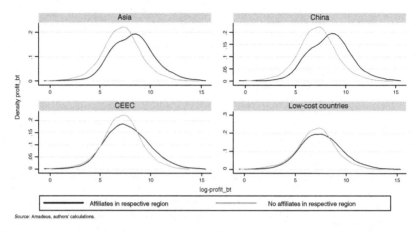

Source: Amadeus, authors' calculations.

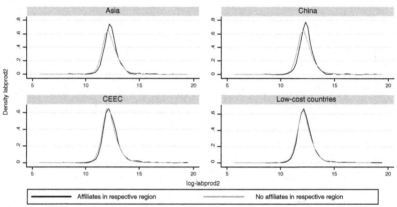

Source: Amadeus, authors' calculations.

Kolmogorov–Smirnov test – distribution of firms with affiliates in geographic region below dominates distribution of the rest of the sample

	Turnover	Employment	Profits	Labour productivity (va/empl)	Labour productivity (turnover/empl)
Asia	0.997	1.000	0.999	0.988	0.781
China	1.000	1.000	0.997	0.984	0.711
CEEC	0.998	0.897	0.995	1.000	1.000
Low-cost	1.000	1.000	0.995	0.022	0.992

Figure 4.6 (*cont.*)

5   Dynamics

Having established that firms with foreign affiliates perform better than other firms in terms of a number of characteristics in a static context, this section now takes a brief look at dynamic issues. What is the pattern of entry and exit among such MNEs in the euro area countries, and how

Table 4.8 *Exit, survival and newcomer rate for the United Kingdom, France, Germany and Italy (2003 and 2006)*

	All firms	MNEs in 2003[1]	MNEs in 2006
		United Kingdom	
Exit rate	6.83	5.93	
Survival rate	93.17	94.07	100.00
Newcomer rate start-ups[2]	0.35		0.36
Newcomer rate new-bigs	3.10		12.04
		France	
Exit rate	15.65	11.04	
Survival rate	84.35	88.96	100.00
Newcomer rate start-ups	0.09		0.47
Newcomer rate new-bigs	0.74		17.41
		Germany	
Exit rate	18.52	15.87	
Survival rate	81.48	84.13	100.00
Newcomer rate start-ups	0.38		1.67
Newcomer rate new-bigs	3.06		34.11
		Italy	
Exit rate	13.06	12.63	
Survival rate	86.94	87.37	100.00
Newcomer rate start-ups	2.32		8.21
Newcomer rate new-bigs	7.24		75.14

Notes:
[1] 2003 = base year.
[2] New market entries are of two types: 'start-ups' and 'new-bigs'. If their date of incorporation is more recent than 2003, we classify them as 'start-ups'. If their date of incorporation precedes 2003, however, but they were sampled only in the 2006 release while meeting the requirements to be sampled in 2003, we classify them as 'new-bigs'.

does it compare with the picture in the United Kingdom? Table 4.8 provides a first look at such firm dynamics. The first column provides figures on the entry, exit and survival of all firms in the respective country between 2003 and 2006. It is notable here that the overall rate of exit in Germany, France and Italy is about 15 per cent – in other words, around a sixth of the firms that existed in 2003 had exited by 2006.[10] During the same time, the entry rate (i.e. the share of firms that exist in 2006 but did not exist in 2003) differed markedly across the three countries. The United Kingdom displays a slightly different performance, with a far lower rate of exit but also the lowest rate of new firm entry over the 2003–6 period.

[10] These rates are broadly in line with earlier work for Germany and Italy by Wagner (1994) and Audretsch *et al.* (1999). These papers consider only the exit rates of new firms, however.

Columns 2 and 3 of the table look in more detail at entry and exit among firms with foreign affiliates. For Germany, we find that 16 per cent of MNEs that were in the sample in 2003 had exited by 2006. Only 2 per cent of the MNEs that existed in 2006 had not been in the data in 2003, however. While the exit rate is lower for MNEs than for firms in general (column 1), this is also true for the rate of new entry by firms with foreign affiliates. A similar pattern can be observed for the two other euro area countries as well as for the United Kingdom: rates of both entry and exit are lower for firms with foreign affiliates than for the economy overall, but the rate of exit of MNEs is well in excess of the rate of new entry by those types of firms. The lower exit rate for MNEs echoes similar findings on comparisons between the survival and exit of domestic firms and MNEs by Görg and Strobl (2003) for Ireland and Bernard and Jensen (2007) for the United States. Comparisons of entry rates for these types of firms are, to the best of our knowledge, not available in the literature.

The table presents only a first look at the patterns of entry and exit among multinational firms – an issue that as yet has not received much attention in the academic literature. While it is beyond the scope of the current chapter to provide further analysis of this, it is a topic we will be considering in future research. A number of questions seem to be fruitful avenues for further research. What explains the low rates of entry among firms with foreign affiliates? Is there evidence that firms start as purely domestic firms or exporters and only after a certain period start investing abroad? What are the characteristics of new entrants and exiting firms? Finally, what are the contributions from this high level of dynamism among MNEs to overall productivity growth in the economy?

6   Conclusions

This chapter has analysed firm-level data for euro area countries in order to chart patterns of trade and investment activity among firms. The analysis, essentially, has taken a snapshot of the data in 2004 to do so. We have looked at the export activity of firms in order to position our chapter in the larger recent international literature on this topic, but the main focus has been on examining activities in terms of multinational operations abroad. In this respect we have moved into largely uncharted territory, as this has not received that much attention in the literature to date. We have investigated what share of euro area country firms locate affiliates abroad, how many subsidiaries they have and in which countries they locate. We have also looked at the characteristics of firms that go abroad relative to those that do not, and whether these characteristics are different for MNEs depending on the magnitude and location of their foreign operations.

Our exploratory findings have unearthed a number of interesting facts. While only a small share of euro area firms locate affiliates abroad, these firms account for over-proportionally large shares of output, employments and profits in their home countries. We have also found that, on average, firms that establish affiliates abroad are larger, more profitable and more productive than firms that do not. While this to some extent mirrors findings in the previous literature (e.g. Helpman *et al.*, 2004, and Girma *et al.*, 2004), we have also shown that there are performance premia (in terms of size, profits and productivity) for MNEs with a large number of affiliates abroad relative to those with a small number.

In terms of locations, we have found that MNEs generally have affiliates in more than one country. Highly productive MNEs tend to go to more distant destinations in larger percentages than poor-performing MNEs, which prefer to locate their affiliates within the European region. Among the highly productive MNEs the United States is the top destination, whereas other MNEs favour euro area countries, France and Germany in particular. Furthermore, we have found that MNEs that locate in low-income countries, in particular in Asia, are larger and more productive than those that do not locate in these regions/countries.

Our analysis is a first step towards a better understanding of multinational activity at the firm level, and the implications for firm characteristics and, ultimately, economic activity in the country overall. It suggests that there is substantial heterogeneity across different firm types, not only among domestic firms, exporters and MNEs, as recognised in the literature to date, but also in the much smaller subgroup of MNEs in which firm characteristics are significantly related to patterns of the magnitude and location of their investment abroad. This needs to be recognised by policy-makers in their attempts to assess the possible implications of increasing levels of outward investment by euro area firms.

The research reported in this chapter in some sense, perhaps, raises more questions than it answers. Why do some firms choose to have only small levels of foreign investment, while other firms set up a large number of affiliates? Why do different types of firms set up in different countries? What does this tell us about the importance of sunk costs of investment, which are highlighted in the recent theoretical literature on heterogeneous firm models? How does the pattern of foreign investment change over time, and how is it shaped by external factors? And, perhaps most crucially, what are the implications of these activities for the parent firm and the home country overall? These are important questions, which can fruitfully be addressed in further research based on the data used in this chapter.

References

Arnold, J., and K. Hussinger (2005), 'Exports versus FDI in German Manufacturing: Firm Performance and Participation in International Markets', mimeo, World Bank, Washington, DC.

Audretsch, D., E. Santarelli and M. Vivarelli (1999), 'Does Startup Size Influence the Likelihood of Survival?', in D. Audretsch and R. Thurik (eds.), *Innovation, Industry Evolution and Employment* (Cambridge: Cambridge University Press), 280–96.

Bernard, A., J. Eaton, J. Jensen and S. Kortum (2003), 'Plants and Productivity in International Trade', *American Economic Review*, 93, 4, 1268–90.

Bernard, A., and J. Jensen (1999), 'Exceptional Exporter Performance: Cause, Effect or Both?', *Journal of International Economics*, 47, 1, 1–25.

—— (2007), 'Firm Structure, Multinationals, and Manufacturing Plant Deaths', *Review of Economics and Statistics*, 89, 2, 193–204.

Bernard, A., J. Jensen and P. Schott (2005), 'Importers, Exporters, and Multinationals: A Portrait of Firms in the US that Trade Goods', Working Paper no. 11404, National Bureau of Economic Research, Cambridge, MA.

Bernard, A., and J. Wagner (2001), 'Export Entry and Exit by German Firms', *Weltwirtschaftliches Archiv*, 137, 1, 105–23.

Castellani, D. (2002), 'Export Behaviour and Productivity Growth: Evidence from Italian Manufacturing Firms', *Weltwirtschaftliches Archiv*, 138, 4, 605–28.

Castellani, D., and A. Zanfei (2004), 'Internationalisation, Innovation and Productivity: How Do Firms Differ in Italy?', mimeo, University of Urbino.

Clerides, S. K., S. Lach and J. R. Tybout (1998), 'Is Learning by Exporting Important? Microdynamic Evidence from Colombia, Mexico and Morocco', *Quarterly Journal of Economics*, 113, 3, 903–47.

Davis, S. J., and J. C. Haltiwanger (1992), 'Gross Job Creation, Gross Job Destruction, and Employment Reallocation', *Quarterly Journal of Economics* 107, 3, 819–63.

Davis, S. J., J. C. Haltiwanger and S. Schuh (1996), *Job Creation and Destruction* (Cambridge, MA: MIT Press).

Delgado, M., J. C. Farinas and S. Ruano (2002), 'Firm Productivity and Export Markets: A Non-parametric Approach', *Journal of International Economics*, 57, 2, 397–422.

Eaton, J., S. Kortum and F. Kramarz (2004), 'An Anatomy of International Trade: Evidence from French Firms', mimeo, New York University.

Girma, S., H. Görg and E. Strobl (2004), 'Exports, International Investment, and Plant Performance: Evidence from a Non-parametric Test', *Economics Letters*, 83, 3, 317–24.

Girma, S., R. Kneller and M. Pisu (2005), 'Exports versus FDI: An Empirical Test', *Weltwirtschaftliches Archiv*, 141, 2, 193–218.

Görg, H., and E. Strobl (2003), 'Footloose Multinationals?', *The Manchester School*, 71, 1, 1–19.

Greenaway, D., and R. Kneller (2008), 'Exporting, Productivity and Agglomeration', forthcoming in *European Economic Review*.

Head, K., and J. Ries (2003), 'Heterogeneity and the Foreign Direct Investment versus Export Decision of Japanese Manufacturers', *Journal of the Japanese and International Economies*, **17**, 4, 448–67.

Helpman, E., M. Melitz and S. Yeaple (2004), 'Exports versus FDI', *American Economic Review*, **94**, 1, 300–16.

Melitz, M. (2003), 'The Impact of Trade on Aggregate Industry Productivity and Intra-industry Reallocation', *Econometrica*, **71**, 6, 1695–725.

Montagna, C. (2001), 'Efficiency Gaps, Love of Variety and International Trade', *Economica*, **68**, 27–44.

Ottaviano, G., D. Taglioni and F. di Mauro (2007), 'Deeper, Wider and More Competitive? Monetary Integration, Eastern Enlargement and Competitiveness in the European Union', mimeo, European Central Bank, Frankfurt.

Wagner, J. (1994), 'The Post-entry Performance of New Small Firms in German Manufacturing Industries', *Journal of Industrial Economics*, **42**, 2, 141–54.

(2005), 'Exports and Productivity: A Survey of the Evidence from Firm-level Data', Working Paper no. 4, University of Lüneburg.

5 Globalisation and the trade channel in the euro area

Robert Anderton and Filippo di Mauro[1]

1 Introduction

At times since the late 1990s the strong performance of the global economy has appeared to find little correspondence with euro area activity, casting doubts on the strength of the trade channel in the euro area (see figure 5.1). This is a puzzle, given the very open nature of the euro area – at least, as far as its component economies are concerned. Three main questions arise from this finding. First, whether the possible changes in the trade channel are attributable to globalisation, particularly the entry of new global players in world trade, such as China – a factor that is shared by other major developed economies. Second, whether and how the phenomenon relates instead mostly to regional factors, in particular to the interaction between economies participating in the monetary union. Third, whether there are reasons to believe that the phenomenon is bound to persist. This chapter looks at external trade impacts on the euro area and analyses how those impacts are transmitted to the euro area against the background of the various possible structural effects that are related to the ongoing and rapid rise in globalisation. The interaction of globalisation and regional forces represents the main focus.

The chapter analyses, first, the impact of world trade movements on exports outside the euro area. It shows how globalisation seems to be associated with much faster growth in world trade, while the emergence of new global trade players has affected the export market share of the euro area and its constituent countries as well as other major industrialised economies. In terms of the interactions within the euro area, the chapter shows that the ultimate impact of a positive foreign demand shock on the euro area depends on the extent to which the shock translates into internal or external trade. In this context, structural changes related to the globalisation of production processes, most notably the higher import content of

---

[1] Respectively Adviser and Head of Division, External Developments Division, European Central Bank.

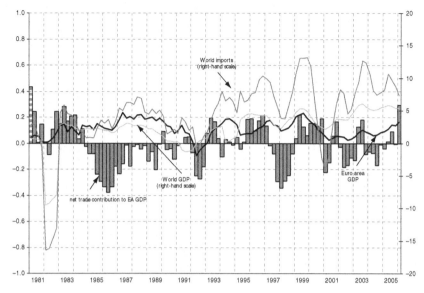

Figure 5.1 World demand and euro area activity
Notes: Index: 1980=100; four-quarter moving average; year-on-year
growth rate.

exports, are found to play an important role, including changes in the
trade impact of exchange rate movements. Throughout the chapter the
analysis is supported by an econometric model of trade in goods outside
the euro area, which is described in the appendix.

One point emphasised in this chapter is that globalisation has brought
many significant benefits to the euro area macroeconomy. From a trade
viewpoint, globalisation has stimulated the growth of extra-euro area
exports, significantly increasing their share of GDP, on account of the
rapid growth in foreign demand. In addition, the rising share of imports
from low-cost countries has reduced costs and prices for both euro area
firms and consumers.

2   Overview of the trade channel of the euro area

The euro area is the sum of very open economies, and intra-regional
transactions within the euro area represent about a half of the total trade
of the euro area. Against this background, and in order to examine the
importance of the trade channel, it is essential to spell out how extra-euro

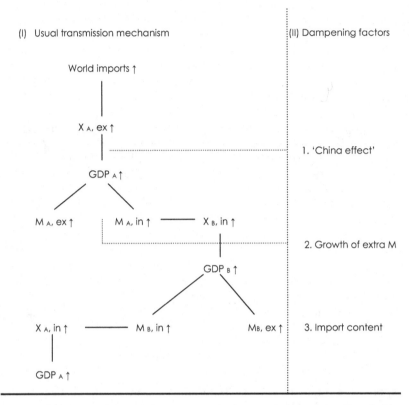

Figure 5.2 External trade impacts and transmission mechanisms for the euro area

area trade interacts with intra-euro area trade and eventually affects the overall activity of the euro area. To help the presentation, figure 5.2 summarises the most critical channels triggered by a positive shock in world imports, distinguishing (1) the usual transmission mechanism (left-hand side) from (2) possible dampening factors (right-hand side). The shock is explained within a two-country EMU framework; it is assumed to impact first one euro area country – country A – and then to spill over to the rest of the euro area, as represented by country B.

The usual transmission mechanism is that higher world imports increase the extra-exports of euro area country A (see left-hand side of figure 5.2). This, in turn, increases economic activity and GDP in country A and stimulates intra-euro area trade spillovers by increasing country A's demand for imports from the other euro area countries. The resulting higher level of activity in these countries (identified as country B) eventually generates additional demand for exports from country A.

With increasing globalisation, however, various factors affect this series of events, as shown on the right-hand side of the figure in the three correspondent points of the chain, perhaps dampening the impact of the foreign shock.

- First comes the 'China effect'. In this the emergence of global trade players such as China causes an increase in world trade, while at the same time shrinking the market shares of the incumbent advanced industrialised economies, such as the euro area (*globalisation linkage 1*). The extent of this loss in share partly depends on how exposed euro area countries are to competition vis-à-vis emerging countries, which, in turn, depends on how similar the export product specialisation of the euro area is to these new competitors.
- The second dampening effect comes from the ongoing growth of extra-euro area imports relative to intra-euro area trade triggered by higher euro area import penetration from low-cost countries outside the euro area (*globalisation linkage 2*). *Ceteris paribus*, this implies a lower potential stimulus feeding through to intra-euro area trade and domestic demand for a given external shock.
- Finally, the actual contribution of the original rise in foreign demand to euro area GDP is also dampened by the rising import content of exports, which tends to lower the net trade contribution per unit of export (*globalisation linkage 3*).

This notwithstanding, it should be emphasised that there are also positive offsetting effects of globalisation that tend to counteract the above dampening factors. For example, despite the decline in export market share, the extra-euro area exports of the euro area have been growing rapidly as a percentage of GDP, on account of the consistently robust growth in foreign demand in recent years. Meanwhile, the rapid growth of extra-euro area imports from low-cost countries is reducing the costs of firms and also benefiting consumers as well as the wider economy of the euro area.

In what follows we examine in some further detail these three linkages, and include an assessment of their quantitative relevance where this is possible, as well as other features of globalisation that may offset some of these effects.

3   Globalisation linkage 1: exports and foreign demand

Against the background of the emergence of low-income countries as major players in world trade, the export market shares of advanced industrialised countries have fallen in recent years, while those of countries such as China have dramatically increased (figure 5.3).

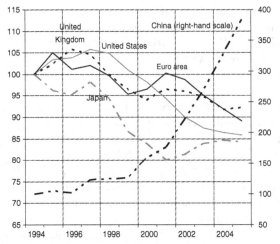

Sources: IMF, Eurostat and ECB calculations.
Note: Last observation refers to December 2005. Export market share is derived as export volumes divided by foreign demand (i.e., a weighted average of import volumes of major trade partners). Shares given in volumes; index: 1994 = 100; annual data.

Figure 5.3 Export market shares

For the euro area – and the United Kingdom – this loss has been less than that for the United States and Japan, and has been mostly concentrated in the last few years, corresponding with the appreciation of the euro. In contrast, the United States and Japan experienced a sharp loss in market share between 1998 and 2002–3, possibly suggesting that the structural adjustment to global trade integration is proceeding at different rates in different countries and regions. Overall, it seems that the losses in export shares occurring across a variety of advanced industrialised countries cannot be fully explained by changes in price competitiveness.[2]

In order to infer whether the emergence of China as a global player in world export markets can be identified as the main reason for such losses for the euro area, we subtract world imports from China from the euro area foreign demand indicator. In other words, we deduct China's exports to the world and use this modified measure of foreign demand as a counterfactual to see what would have happened to the euro area's export market share under this scenario. The result (see figure 5.4) shows that the

---

[2] For further details, see ESCB (2005).

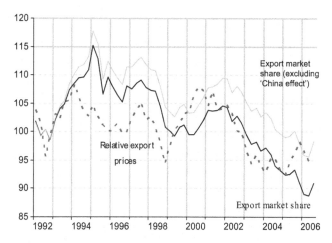

Figure 5.4 China's impact on euro area export market shares
Note: volume index, 1992 = 100.

dynamics of the euro area export market share before 1999 did not change, as China's trade growth was similar to growth in world trade in this period. Between 1999 and 2006, however, which corresponds to the period of the rapid expansion of China's share in world trade, the euro area's market share loss becomes significantly smaller if we take out the impact of China's exports to the world. This indicates that the trade integration of China associated with globalisation may have been a prominent reason for the fall in the euro area's export market share, which is not explained by export price competitiveness effects.

This is also confirmed by an econometric analysis of euro area exports in the appendix, using the modified foreign demand excluding China. By doing so, the negative time trend – which captures the structural, unexplained decrease in euro area market share apparent when using the usual foreign demand indicator including China – becomes statistically insignificant. In other words, the dynamics of euro area exports can now be fully explained by the modified foreign demand measure and changes in relative export prices.

We should remind ourselves, however, that, despite the decline in export market share, the extra-euro area exports of the euro area are growing rapidly as a percentage of GDP, reflecting the persistently robust growth in foreign demand (figure 5.5). Given that these favourable global demand conditions also seem to be at least partly driven by the forces of globalisation, the resulting positive impact on exports tends broadly to

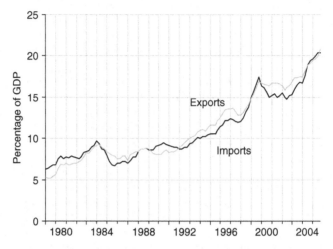

Figure 5.5 Extra-euro area exports and imports as percentage of GDP
Note: quarterly data; values.

offset the dampening effect of the loss in share (see the appendix for
further details).

Having identified that a 'China effect' accounts by and large for the loss
in export market share, we can provide further insights into the mechanisms behind this loss by assessing the extent to which Chinese exports in
terms of their sectoral composition compete directly with the euro area,
and at the same time investigating how the euro area is adjusting its export
structure to respond to this competitive challenge.

Drawing from research detailed elsewhere,[3] we can conclude that
results on the above are rather mixed. On the one hand, the euro area as
a whole, despite being relatively specialised in medium-/high-tech exports,
appears to be less open to direct competition from China than other major
trading partners are, such as the United States (table 5.1).

On the other hand, the loss in export market share of the euro area is
the result of a relatively diverse performance across euro area countries
(see figure 5.6 for selected euro area countries), with the export share
losses of some of them weighing rather heavily on the euro area aggregate.
Italy, in particular, has experienced significant export market share losses
since 1995, together with France (albeit to a lesser extent), Portugal
and Greece. Meanwhile, many of the other euro area countries have

---

[3] See, for instance, Baumann and di Mauro (2007).

Table 5.1 *Balassa index of revealed comparative advantage of exports across regions (index based on dollar values, average 1993–2004)*

	Euro area	United States	United Kingdom	Japan	China	Other emerging Asia	CEEC
Memo item:							
Share in total world exports of goods	17.5	12.0	5.0	8.6	4.4	11.7	5.3
High-technology industries	0.9	1.4	1.4	1.3	1.0	1.7	0.3
Medium-/high-technology industries	1.2	1.1	1.0	1.5	0.6	0.6	0.9
Medium-/low-technology industries	0.9	0.7	0.7	0.9	0.7	0.9	1.9
Low-technology industries	0.9	0.8	0.9	0.3	1.6	1.0	1.2

Notes: A value higher than one indicates a comparative advantage in that sector. Euro area exports exclude intra-euro area trade. Total exports exclude exports of energy-related products.

Sources: Centre d'Etudes Prospectives et d'Information Internationals' (CEPII's) CHELEM database and ECB calculations.

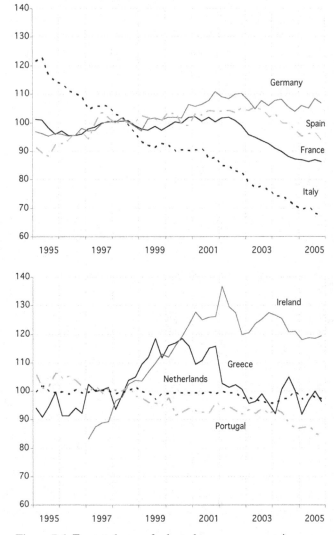

Figure 5.6 Export shares of selected euro area countries

maintained broadly stable export market shares or even increased them (particularly Ireland and Germany). Although movements in market shares seem to be explained partly by relative export price competitive-ness, with Germany gaining competitiveness and Italy losing competitive-ness, the overall correlation between changes in export market share and relative export prices is not particularly strong at the euro area country

Table 5.2 *Revealed comparative advantage of exports for euro area, euro area countries and China*

	High-technology industries	Medium-/high-technology industries	Medium-/low-technology industries	Low-technology industries	Low-technology industries: of which textiles, clothing and footwear
Euro area (intra + extra)	0.7	1.2	1.0	1.0	0.9
Germany	0.7	1.4	1.0	0.7	0.5
France	1.0	1.1	1.0	0.9	0.7
Italy	0.5	1.2	1.1	1.2	2.1
Netherlands	1.1	0.8	1.0	1.2	0.6
Spain	0.4	1.3	1.2	1.0	0.9
Ireland	1.9	0.8	0.2	0.9	0.2
Belgium/ Luxembourg	0.5	1.0	1.4	1.1	0.9
Finland	0.9	0.8	1.2	1.2	0.2
Austria	0.5	1.2	1.2	1.0	0.8
Portugal	0.4	0.9	0.8	1.6	3.6
Greece	0.3	0.4	1.5	2.0	2.9
China	1.0	0.6	0.7	1.6	3.6

Sources: CEPII's CHELEM database and ECB calculations.

level. This suggests that some individual euro area countries may have been more strongly affected than others by globalisation, possibly due to their export specialisation exposing them more directly to competition from China.

To check this hypothesis, we analysed indicators of revealed comparative advantage[4] (table 5.2) computed as ratios of the sectoral specialisation of a country with respect to the world (i.e. an index greater than one indicates a revealed comparative advantage in that sector). Overall, the euro area specialises in medium-tech industries, and its revealed comparative advantages are largely concentrated in sectors in which China is still relatively weak. This is not true, however, for all euro area countries. In particular, Greece, Portugal and, to a lesser extent, Italy appear to be rather strongly specialised in low- and medium-/low-technology sectors (particularly textiles), in which China is gaining predominance, largely because of its substantially lower labour costs and recent accession to the World Trade Organization.

---

[4] See ECB (2006) for details on the calculation and pitfalls of such indicators.

Overall, on this first possible globalisation linkage, one can conclude that the China effect has certainly been relevant in explaining overall export market share losses. Given the sectoral specialisation of the euro area as a whole, however, the euro area has been less exposed to direct competition from China than other countries, such as the United States. At the same time, the euro area has been somewhat slower in moving towards higher-tech sectors. More specifically, a number of euro area countries still appear to be lagging behind in terms of adjusting their export structure in line with the global redistribution of comparative advantage, which may be a sign of rigidities in product and labour markets.

4   Globalisation linkage 2: the strength of intra- relative to extra-euro area trade

From 1995 to 2006 both intra- and extra-euro area imports of manufactured goods showed robust growth. At 6 per cent per annum, however, the growth rate of extra-euro area imports exceeded that of intra-euro area imports (which grew at a robust 5 per cent per annum, nevertheless), thus leading to a decline in the ratio of intra- to extra-euro area imports. This might be considered somewhat surprising, considering that monetary union theory had predicted a very strong boost to intra-regional trade (for example, the 'Rose effect', as in Rose, 2000) and is at odds with developments in relative prices. For instance, relative volumes remained fairly stable from 1999 to 2001, when relative prices moved strongly in favour of intra-area transactions following the euro depreciation. Overall, for the whole sample period, figure 5.7 shows that there was a decline in the intra/extra import volumes ratio between 1995 and 2006, while the relative price of the two sources of imports in 2006 was very similar to what it was in 1995, implying that a structural trend decline is taking place that is not explained by relative prices.

Clearly, globalisation forces were even stronger than regional ones. And there was good reason for that. As global trade integration proceeded and the presence of low-cost suppliers became more predominant, there was an obvious convenience for individual euro area economies to shift part of their imports away from traditional high-cost import suppliers – including, therefore, euro area import suppliers – and towards low-cost economies, most notably eastern Europe and emerging Asia (particularly China).

This process has involved all suppliers of imports to the euro area. As figure 5.8 shows, in the past decade the shares of low-cost countries in euro area imports of manufactures – particularly those of China and the new EU member states – have increased considerably, accompanied by a

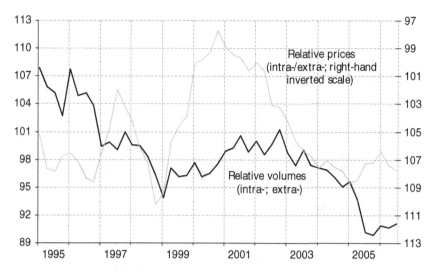

Figure 5.7 Intra- relative to extra-euro area imports of manufactured goods
Note: index 2002 Q1=100; monthly data.

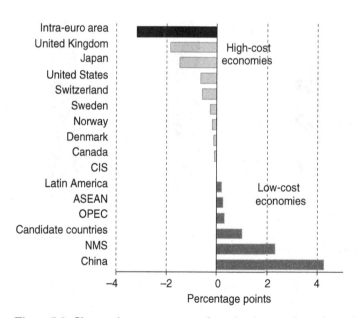

Figure 5.8 Changes in euro area manufacturing import shares by region/country of origin (1995–2005)
Note: Percentage point changes.

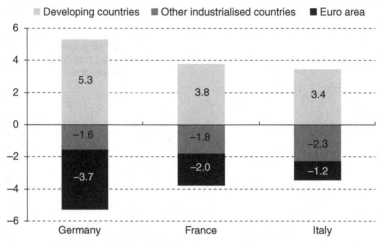

Sources: Eurostat and ECB calculations.
Note: Percentage point changes. Intra-euro area trade is defined as the average
of intra-euro area imports and intra-euro area exports.

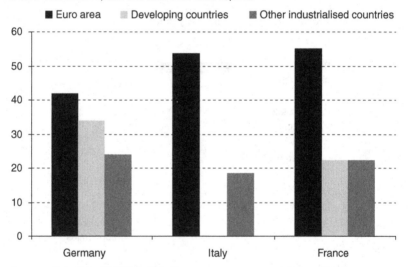

Sources: Eurostat and ECB calculations.
Notes: Based on trade in value terms. Share of euro area imports from a given
country/region divided by total (intra- plus extra-euro area) imports.

Figure 5.9 Import shares by region for Germany, France and Italy

loss in the import shares of both intra-euro area import suppliers as well as high-cost extra-euro area importers (the United States, Japan and the United Kingdom). Of course, this is also simply reflecting the flip side of the loss in export market share of the major advanced industrialised countries described in section 1.

Among euro area countries (figure 5.9), Germany appears to be more open to extra-euro area imports than France and Italy. Germany's import penetration from developing low-cost countries is particularly strong (above 30 per cent of total intra- plus extra-euro area imports), which can be explained partly by its geographical proximity to eastern European countries, particularly the NMS, which has encouraged an internationalisation of production processes vis-à-vis these countries and Germany.

In conclusion, alongside the trade-creating effect of EMU, globalisation and the strengthening of international competition have greatly influenced recent developments in euro area imports. In particular, imports of manufactures from low-cost countries are seen to have displaced part of the imports from both intra-euro area and high-cost extra-euro area importers. Among the low-cost trading partners, China and the NMS stand out as having recorded substantial growth in import shares in the euro area over a wide range of manufacturing products during this period. These developments, while admittedly boosting the welfare of euro area consumers, have, on the other hand, very probably affected the transmission of foreign demand shocks to euro area domestic demand, by weakening some of the potential intra-trade spillovers.

Going forward, the persistence of this effect is obviously contingent upon the extent to which import penetration from low-cost countries stops increasing. The evidence available, however, suggests that the process is far from over, thus implying that the globalisation linkage identified here is bound to persist for a while yet (figure 5.10).

5   Globalisation linkage 3: net trade and the import content of exports

The rapid rise in extra-euro area imports documented above appears to be related to two main broad causes: first, the increased penetration of cheaper common goods from low-cost countries; and, second, the acceleration of the process of the internationalisation of production, which increasingly involves low-wage economies. In this section, we look at the way such new trends have affected interactions between exports, imports, GDP and the net trade contribution to GDP (figure 5.11) and, eventually, have changed the ways in which the international environment impacts on the euro area. Two points seem particularly relevant. First, the

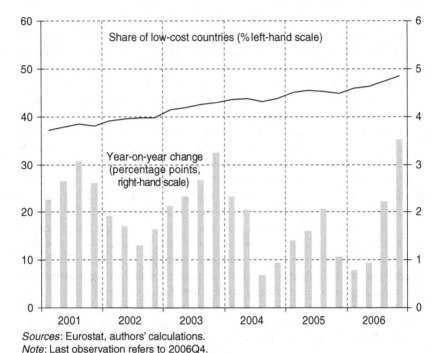

Sources: Eurostat, authors' calculations.
Note: Last observation refers to 2006Q4.

Figure 5.10 Share of euro area manufacturing imports from low-cost countries
Note: Values in euros.

euro area experienced an increase in the correlation of export and import growth during the 1990s. This is possibly due to a higher share of production processes being delocalised abroad, and to the related additional trade flows, partly via an increase in imported intermediate inputs. Second, the magnitude of the euro area's net trade contribution to GDP has fallen over the past quarter of a century (with the exception of the outlier in the final quarter of 2006), which, again, is consistent with exports and imports moving more closely together.

One possible implication of the trend increase in the internationalisation of production is that production offshoring may have had a negative spillover on economic activity, as it could have reduced the value added of export activities by increasing the reliance of euro area exporters on imported intermediate inputs. Box 6 in ESCB (2005) shows that the import content of exports (which is the mirror image of the value added per unit of export) – measured as the long-run elasticity of imports with respect to a one-unit increase in exports – rose for the euro area from 38 per cent in 1995 to around

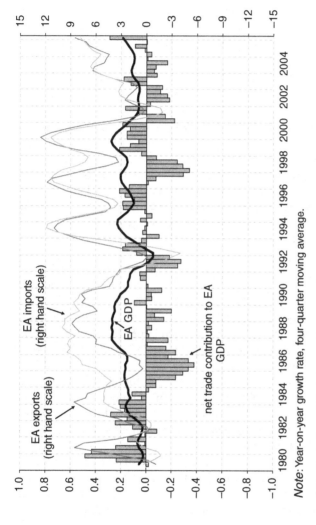

Note: Year-on-year growth rate, four-quarter moving average.

Figure 5.11 Evolution of the euro area's exports, imports, net trade and GDP

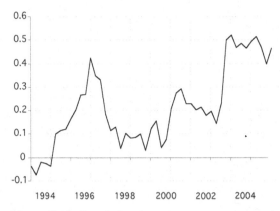

Figure 5.12 Correlation between extra-euro area export and import volumes of goods

44 per cent in 2000. Furthermore, this rise in the import intensity of exports was almost entirely due to trade external to the European Union, as the import intensity of internal EU trade did not change much over this period.[5]

This is further confirmed for the more recent period by figure 5.12, which shows how the correlation between the extra-euro area export and import volumes of goods has increased over time (see also Stirböck, 2006, for evidence that the marginal import content of German exports has increased significantly over time). Globalisation and the internationalisation of production – which partly explains the rise in imported intermediate inputs – has also boosted exports as well, however.[6] As a result, given that the share of exports in GDP is now much larger (figure 5.5), the net impact of a 1 per cent increase in exports on GDP growth may have remained roughly constant for the euro area.

Another aspect of this globalisation-related phenomenon is its possible effects on the trade impact of exchange rate movements. Given that the import content of exports is rising over time, one would expect import prices to become an increasingly important component of exporters' costs. If this is the case, there may be smaller losses in export price competitiveness in response to an appreciation of the exchange rate compared to the past, which, in turn, mitigates the negative impact of a euro appreciation on export volumes. This is because an appreciation will reduce the cost of imported inputs, and exporters can reduce their prices

[5] As the data related to the period 1995–2000, the EU data exclude the NMS that joined the European Union in 2004.
[6] For the euro area, the share of (intra- plus extra-euro area) exports in GDP rose from 23 per cent in 1995 to 30 per cent in 2000.

to partly offset the loss in competitiveness from the appreciation. This is confirmed by export price equation (2′) in the appendix, which shows that import prices are indeed an important cost component of export prices.

6   Conclusions

This chapter has examined the extent to which globalisation linkages may have dampened the impact of positive foreign shocks on euro area economic activity. It needs to be emphasised, however, that the overall impact of globalisation on the euro area has been positive. From a trade perspective, globalisation has contributed significantly to the robust growth of extra-euro area exports by stimulating world demand, while euro area firms and consumers have benefited from the lower costs and prices associated with the rising share of imports from low-cost countries, such as China and the NMS.

Nevertheless, it has been shown that the globalisation linkages under consideration have been, and still are, very strong, tending to overshadow the impact of regionalisation. A precise quantification of the net impact arising from the three globalisation linkages considered – for a given positive world import shock – is, clearly, very hard to ascertain. It has been shown, however, that all three of the linkages may have been important factors in explaining a perceived weakening of the trade link in the last few years. Going forward, globalisation linkages 1 and 2 appear to remain the most relevant, as the processes out of which they emerge – i.e. the entry of new global trade players and the increased penetration of low-cost imports, respectively – are still very much ongoing. As for the third linkage – the increase in the import content of exports – it is likely to have the least impact, as the process is taking place within the ongoing dynamism of world exports.

Appendix

An econometric assessment of extra-euro area trade in goods[7]

This appendix describes some key extra-euro area trade elasticities as estimated by ECB staff using econometric techniques and quarterly data over the period from the first quarter of 1993 to the third quarter of 2006. The overall framework consists of sixteen econometric equations and identities for goods and services based on extra-euro area trade data using a combination of Eurostat's External Trade Statistics as well as

---

[7] All the equations reported in the appendix were estimated by Konstantins Benkovskis (while at the ECB on secondment from the Bank of Latvia) and Laurent Maurin of the ECB.

Table 5A.1 *Extra-euro area trade in goods: estimates of long-run elasticities*

Volumes		Prices[1]	
Exports of goods[2]		Exports of goods	
Foreign demand	Relative prices	Domestic costs	Competitors' prices
1.00	−0.76	0.52	0.48
Imports of manufacturing products		Imports of manufacturing products	
Domestic demand	Relative price	Domestic prices	Foreign costs
1.90	−0.76	0.30	0.70
Imports of non-energy commodities		Imports of non-energy commodities	
Domestic demand	Relative prices	Domestic prices	Foreign costs
0.70	−0.86	0.39	0.61
Imports of energy		Imports of energy	
Domestic demand	Relative prices	Domestic prices	Foreign costs
0.95	−0.10	0.13	0.87

Notes:
[1] The degree of exchange rate pass-through is given by the 'competitors' prices' elasticity in the export price equation and by the 'foreign costs' parameter in the import price equation.
[2] The exports of goods equation includes a negative time trend.
Source: ECB.

the ECB's balance of payments data. In this appendix, however, our focus is on the econometric results for export and import volumes and prices for trade in goods. In addition, imports of goods are subdivided into manufacturing goods, non-oil commodities and energy products. Extra-euro area trade volumes of goods have been regressed against measures of demand and relative prices, while extra-euro area export and import prices are determined by a weighted average of costs and competitors' prices (the latter representing pricing-to-market).[8] The long-run parameters of the equations are reported in table 5A.1.

Extra-euro area export volumes of goods

Extra-euro area export volumes of goods (x_ttt_r) are estimated using an export-weighted volume of world imports as the foreign demand variable

[8] A single-equation framework is estimated with ordinary least squares, and all econometric equations are determined by a combination of long-run relationships, determined by an error correction term, and short-term dynamics. The equations are estimated over the period from the first quarter of 1993 to the third quarter of 2006 on a quarterly basis.

(*fd*), and extra-euro area export prices divided by the weighted competitor's export prices as the relative price competitiveness variable (*rxp*). In the long run, a unit elasticity is imposed on the foreign demand term, while the long-run elasticity of exports for relative export prices is 0.76 (equation 1).[9] A time trend (*trend*) is also included in the export of goods equation, however, which has a negative and statistically significant coefficient, indicating that the euro area's export market share experienced a trend decline over the sample period that cannot be explained by variations in price competitiveness. Although there are a range of estimates, the downward trend points to an average annual loss of up to 0.9 percentage points in euro area market share, which is usually interpreted as the effect of China's integration into world trade and seems related to the ongoing process of globalisation.[10]

$$\Delta x\_ttt\_r = \underset{\substack{(-5.21)\\[0.000]}}{-0.252} \cdot (x\_ttt\_r_{-1} - fd_{-1}) - \underset{\substack{(-4.13)\\[0.001]}}{0.192} \cdot rxp_{-1} - \underset{\substack{(-3.40)\\[0.001]}}{0.00057} \cdot trend +$$

$$+ \underset{\substack{(7.67)\\[0.000]}}{0.810} \cdot \Delta fd - \underset{\substack{(-1.95)\\[0.057]}}{0.153} \cdot \Delta rxp + \underset{\substack{(3.35)\\[0.002]}}{0.038} \cdot d951 - \underset{\substack{(-4.93)\\[0.000]}}{0.037} \cdot (d953 - d953_{-1})$$

$$+ \underset{\substack{(2.99)\\[0.004]}}{0.032} \cdot d964 + \underset{\substack{(3.38)\\[0.001]}}{0.800} \tag{1}$$

$R^2 = 0.748$

$DW = 1.83$

Next, we investigate whether China explains euro area market share losses by excluding the effect of China's trade with the world. We can do this by a simple elimination of China's exports to the world – excluding China's exports to the euro area – from the foreign demand indicator (in other words, we exclude world imports supplied by China).[11] We then re-estimate equation (1) using this modified indicator of foreign demand. Most of the coefficients in the modified equation are similar to the basic model; in particular, the long-run elasticity of export volumes to relative export prices is virtually the same. The principal change occurs to the estimated coefficient on the time trend, which is now *not* statistically significant at the 5 per cent level (and is also much smaller in magnitude, indicating a loss in share of only 0.4 pp per annum). In other words, the dynamics of euro area exports can now be better explained by the modified foreign

---

[9] The terms *d951*, *d953* and *d964* are dummy variables.
[10] In all equations, ( ) = t-values, [ ] = p-values.
[11] All calculations are made in constant prices.

demand indicator and by changes in relative export prices. This indicates that the trade integration of China associated with globalisation is a prominent reason for the loss in market share of the euro area proxied by the negative time trend in equation (1). Nevertheless, strong global demand conditions – which seem to be at least partly driven by globalisation forces – have resulted in strong growth in euro area exports despite the loss in export share. Using the National Institute of Economic and Social Research's Global Econometric Model, removing the impact of China from 2000 onwards would lead to a loss in foreign demand of between 5 and 6 per cent after six years. Meanwhile, the negative time trend in equation (1) above implies a loss in market share of around 5.4 per cent (i.e. 0.9 per cent per annum over six years). Therefore, the positive and negative effects on euro area exports seem, roughly, to offset each other.

Extra-euro area export prices

Export prices of goods (x_ttt_d) are specified as partly depending on costs (ppi) and partly on competitors' export prices (cxp) – i.e., pricing-to-market – with the estimated parameters suggesting that extra-euro area exporters give roughly equal weight to these two components, implying that a 1 per cent increase in either costs or competitors' prices brings about a 0.5 per cent increase in export prices in the long run (equation (2)). As competitors' prices include the impact of changes in exchange rates, the parameters indicate that the pass-through of changes in the effective exchange rate of the euro to extra-euro area export prices of goods is around 50 per cent. This implies that euro area export profit margins are reduced (increased) in response to an appreciation (depreciation), thereby limiting the impact on export price competitiveness of movements in exchange rates. In the short run, export prices also depend on changes in the nominal effective exchange rate (een).

$$\Delta x\_ttt\_d = \underset{\substack{(-5.03) \\ [0.000]}}{-0.110} \cdot x\_ttt\_d_{-1} + \underset{\substack{(4.03) \\ [0.000]}}{0.052} \cdot cxp_{-1} + (0.110 - 0.052) \cdot ppi_{-1} -$$

$$\underset{\substack{(-12.0) \\ [0.000]}}{-0.282} \cdot \Delta een + \underset{\substack{(6.23) \\ [0.000]}}{0.511} \cdot \Delta ppi + \underset{\substack{(4.44) \\ [0.000]}}{0.018} \cdot d001 + \underset{\substack{(3.46) \\ [0.001]}}{0.014} \cdot d951 + \underset{\substack{(4.02) \\ [0.000]}}{0.245} \quad (2)$$

$$R^2 = 0.872$$

$$DW = 2.11$$

In order to examine the impacts of globalisation and the rising import content of exports, we investigate the specific role of extra-euro area import prices as a component of producers' costs by estimating an alternative version of equation (2). In the alternative specification, domestic producer prices are replaced by two variables, which determine domestic costs: extra-euro area import prices (m_ttt_uvx) and domestic unit labour costs (ula).[12] As in equation (2), the homogeneity restriction is applied – i.e. the sum of the long-run coefficients for import prices, unit labour costs and competitors' export prices is imposed to unity.[13]

$$\Delta x\_ttt\_d = \underset{\substack{(-4.36)\\ [0.000]}}{-0.101} \cdot x\_ttt\_d_{-1} + \underset{\substack{(3.11)\\ [0.003]}}{0.038} \cdot m\_ttt\_uvx_{-1} + \underset{\substack{(4.37)\\ [0.000]}}{0.040} \cdot ula_{-1} +$$

$$+ \left(0.101 - 0.038 - 0.040\right) \cdot cpx_{-1} - \underset{\substack{(-6.26)\\ [0.000]}}{0.184} \cdot \Delta een + \underset{\substack{(6.92)\\ [0.000]}}{0.202} \cdot \Delta m\_ttt\_uvx$$

$$+ \underset{\substack{(2.89)\\ [0.006]}}{0.012} \cdot d001 + \underset{\substack{(3.85)\\ [0.000]}}{0.015} \cdot d951 + \underset{\substack{(4.37)\\ [0.000]}}{0.295} \; (2')$$

$$R^2 = 0.879$$

$$DW = 1.66$$

According to equation (2'), the long-run coefficient on extra-euro area import prices is 0.38, which seems to be consistent with the high and rising import component in exports. The long-run elasticity of export prices for domestic unit labour costs is 0.39. Accordingly, as the sum of long-run coefficients is imposed to unity, the long-run elasticity on competitors' export prices, indicating the degree of pricing to market, declines to 0.23. This result is significantly smaller than in equation (2), as domestic producer costs are now connected to exchange rate movements via import price changes. Nonetheless, equation (2') still implies that the loss (gain) in price competitiveness due to an exchange rate appreciation (depreciation) is one-half of the change in the exchange rate as euro appreciation (depreciation) also means a reduction (increase) of producers' costs via lower (higher) import prices.[14] The loss in profits is much smaller in the case of an appreciation, however,

---

[12] We use alternative variables to the producer price index (PPI) when including import prices in the export price equation as the PPI is directly affected by import prices.

[13] According to the Wald test, we cannot reject the hypothesis of long-run homogeneity (p-value = 0.950).

[14] In equation (2) the long-run elasticity on the euro exchange rate (via competitors' export prices) is 0.48. In equation (2') the effect of the exchange rate on export prices goes through two channels: long-run elasticity of 0.23 on competitors' export prices, and elasticity of 0.38 on import prices, which have a long-run elasticity of about 0.7 on the euro exchange rate: $0.23 + (0.38 \times 0.7) = 0.50$.

as costs are reduced by the reduction in import prices caused by the appreciation.

Extra-euro area import volumes

The three categories of import volumes are all specified as depending on total final expenditure – i.e. the domestic activity variable – and the respective relative price variable (competitiveness) – i.e. the relative import price of manufacturing goods, non-oil commodities, the price of energy imports and the relative import price of services. In equation (3), the long-run elasticity of extra-euro area manufacturing import volumes (m_man_r) to domestic activity (tfe) significantly exceeds one, while the relative price elasticity (rmp) is approximately 0.8. Meanwhile, the estimated long-run demand elasticities for non-oil commodities and energy import volumes are less than unity, reflecting the fall over time in the share of non-oil commodities in consumption and the decline in the oil intensity of production.

$$\Delta m\_man\_r = - \underset{\substack{(-1.81) \\ [0.077]}}{0.158} \cdot m\_man\_r_{-1} + \underset{\substack{(1.71) \\ [0.094]}}{0.299} \cdot tfe_{-1} - \underset{\substack{(-1.78) \\ [0.082]}}{0.120} \cdot rmp_{-1} +$$

$$+ \underset{\substack{(2.51) \\ [0.016]}}{0.415} \cdot \Delta x\_ttt\_r + \underset{\substack{(4.73) \\ [0.000]}}{2.592} \cdot \Delta tfe_{-1} - \underset{\substack{(-2.11) \\ [0.040]}}{0.446} \cdot \Delta rmp_{-1} - \underset{\substack{(-2.76) \\ [0.008]}}{0.059} \cdot d951 - \underset{\substack{(-1.69) \\ [0.099]}}{3.638}$$

$$(3)$$

$R^2 = 0.466$

$DW = 2.50$

Extra-euro area import prices

The extra-euro area import price of manufactured goods (m_man_d) depends partly on foreign costs (proxied by competitors' producer prices in euros, cpp) and partly by pricing-to-market (proxied by the euro area producer price index, ppi). The estimated parameters in equation (4) suggest that the long-run exchange rate pass-through for manufacturing import prices is around 70 per cent (cpp).[15] In contrast to highly differentiated manufactured goods, the long-run exchange rate pass-through for more homogeneous and widely traded goods and

[15] Price homogeneity is accepted in the long run – i.e. the sum of the long-run coefficients for domestic and external prices is restricted to one – while a time trend is included to represent increases in product quality over time. The results and estimated elasticities are similar to those reported by Anderton (2003), who estimates that the exchange rate pass-through to manufacturing import prices is in the range of 50–70 per cent.

commodities such as energy is much closer to unity – i.e. around 87 per cent – while imports of non-energy commodities seem to have a long-run pass-through of approximately 60 per cent (table 5A.1).

$$\Delta m\_man\_d = - \underset{\substack{(-4.38) \\ [0.000]}}{0.277} \cdot m\_man\_d_{-1} + \underset{\substack{(4.94) \\ [0.000]}}{0.195} \cdot cpp_{-1}$$

$$+ (0.277 - 0.195) \cdot ppi_{-1} +$$

$$+ \underset{\substack{(2.26) \\ [0.028]}}{0.00027} \cdot trend + \underset{\substack{(2.46) \\ [0.017]}}{0.457} \cdot \Delta ppi + \underset{\substack{(7.09) \\ [0.000]}}{0.288} \cdot \Delta cpp + \underset{\substack{(4.23) \\ [0.000]}}{0.035} \cdot d001 + \underset{\substack{(4.98) \\ [0.000]}}{0.874}$$

$$(4)$$

$$R^2 = 0.807$$

$$DW = 1.82$$

References

Anderton, R. (2003), 'Extra-euro area manufacturing import prices and exchange rate pass-through', Working Paper no. 219, European Central Bank, Frankfurt.

Anderton, R., F. di Mauro and F. Moneta (2004), 'Understanding the Impact of the External Dimension on the Euro Area: Trade, Capital Flows and Other International Macroeconomic Linkages', Occasional Paper no. 12, European Central Bank, Frankfurt.

Baumann, U., and F. di Mauro (2007), 'Globalisation and Euro Area Trade: Interactions and Challenges', Occasional Paper no. 55, European Central Bank, Frankfurt

ECB (2006), 'Competitiveness and the export performance of the euro area', *Monthly Bulletin*, July, 69–79.

ESCB – Task Force of the Monetary Policy Committee (2005), 'Competitiveness and the Export Performance of the Euro Area', Occasional Paper no. 30, European Central Bank, Frankfurt.

Rose, A. K. (2000), 'One Money, One Market: The Effect of Common Currencies on Trade', *Economic Policy*, **15**, 9–45.

Stirböck, C. (2006), 'How Strong is the Impact of Exports and Other Demand Components on German Import Demand? Evidence from Euro-area and Non-euro-area Imports', Discussion Paper no. 39/2006, Series 1: Economic Studies, Deutsche Bundesbank, Frankfurt.

6   Gauging the labour market effects of international trade openness: an application to the US manufacturing sector

Isabel Vansteenkiste and Paul Hiebert[1]

1   Introduction

The increasing trade integration of emerging markets, in conjunction with rapid technological change, has exerted significant pressures on the labour markets of developed economies in recent decades. It has been argued that increased trade openness has led to the attrition of low-skilled jobs in certain sectors to developing countries, with growing imports of labour-intensive manufactured goods from developing countries accompanied by a fragmentation of production across borders. At the same time, technological change has probably contributed to a sectoral reallocation of production biased against primarily low-skilled workers in developed economies. These two phenomena have become progressively intertwined, given the role of trade in technology diffusion and adoption both *directly* (e.g. through imports of capital goods or convergence in technical efficiency) and *indirectly* (through pressure on firms exposed to trade to innovate).

Regional integration agreements may have amplified the effects of trade on labour market developments as such agreements both create and divert trade, while also implying scale and competition effects that lead to changes in country specialisation (see, for instance, Venables, 2001). In the case of the United States, the North American Free Trade Agreement has led to such regionalisation of trade, and has therefore probably been important in shaping labour market developments, particularly in those sectors most open to trade. Naturally, the impacts of trade openness are likely to be strongest in those sectors most subject to competition, either domestic and foreign – that is, those producing traded goods, such as the manufacturing sector. In the United States, as in other developed economies, the manufacturing sector has exhibited relative sluggishness when assessed alongside overall non-farm employment

---

[1] Respectively Economist, International Policy Analysis Division, and Principal Economist, Euro Area Macroeconomic Division, European Central Bank.

since the mid-1970s (see figure 6.1a). Since the mid-1990s this sluggishness has been correlated with a sizeable expansion in the trade deficit in goods and services (figure 6.1b) along with strong productivity gains (figure 6.1c). At the same time, relatively strong productivity gains in the manufacturing sector compared with the overall economy have only partly been reflected in real compensation per hour in that sector (figure 6.1d). Indeed, while trade in the long run would be expected to produce many benefits, some adjustment costs in certain sectors may be associated with adapting to the challenges presented by globalisation in the shorter term.

In this chapter, we assess the extent to which relative weakness in US manufacturing labour market outcomes has derived from increased trade openness by country origin on the basis of two separate but complementary methodologies. The first methodology provides estimates of the effects of trade on US manufacturing employment through factor content calculations. The second methodology is econometric, quantifying the extent to which relative weakness in US manufacturing labour market outcomes has derived from shocks to trade openness by region on the basis of a sectoral VAR methodology. The two methodologies are complementary. On the one hand, the econometric methodology provides an assessment of trade impacts on the labour market in a framework accounting for interaction across labour market variables, which is important given the increasingly accepted role of international trade in shaping productivity developments by broad region – that is, trade with NAFTA, emerging economies and developed economies. On the other hand, the factor content calculations provide, albeit in a more partial framework and for internationally traded manufactured goods only, estimates of openness by more specific geographical origin.

2   Theoretical predictions and existing empirical estimates

In the long run, trade (along with associated technological gains) would be expected to benefit the population of both emerging and developed economies through more efficient resource allocation, lower prices, greater product choice, pecuniary gains from deepening specialisation and, ultimately, higher living standards. Theoretical predictions, such as Heckscher–Ohlin–Samuelson, Stolper–Samuelson and Ricardian models, would suggest that, as trade liberalisation facilitates international specialisation in production, it should result in higher real aggregate incomes and welfare (OECD, 2005). Indeed, comparative advantage within these theoretical frameworks can arise, given different factor intensities along with relative technology differences. In particular, countries are posited to export

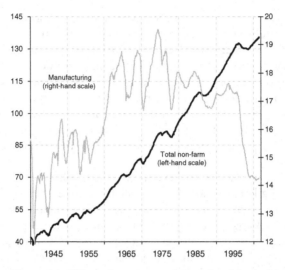

Figure 6.1 US employment, trade, productivity and compensation
(a) US post-war payroll employment (seasonally adjusted)

Figure 6.1 (b) US real trade shares as percentage of real GDP

goods that utilise intensively the factors of production with which they are
relatively abundantly endowed, and import goods that use intensively
factors that are relatively scarce at home.

While growth in international trade would be expected to be welfare-
enhancing in the long run, it probably embeds some adjustment costs

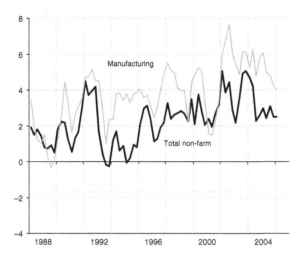

Figure 6.1 (c) US output per hour, year-on-year growth

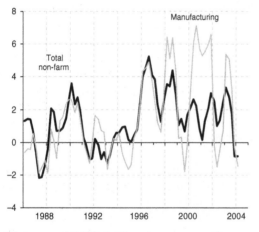

Figure 6.1 (d) US real hourly compensation, year-on-year growth

related to distributional effects associated with the sectoral reallocation of labour. Trade theory would predict adverse effects on sectors with a low-skilled labour content insofar as interaction between emerging and advanced economies is concerned. The ultimate impact of such shifts on particular groups depends ultimately on the interplay of a 'lift all boats' effect versus a 'redistributive' effect (see Bhagwati, 1998). The manufacturing sector may be particularly exposed to frictional unemployment associated with the sectoral reallocation of displaced workers and any associated need for retraining, as job-specific or industry-specific skills are probably more important in manufacturing firms than in service industries, where skills transfer across firms and industries more easily.

Various approaches have been followed in empirically gauging the impacts of international trade on the labour market of developed economies. A first strand of the literature has involved factor content calculations, whereby trade flows are analysed to compute the labour content of imports relative to that of exports to evaluate the net impact of trade on labour markets – such as Baily and Lawrence (2004), Sachs and Shatz (1994) and Wood (1995, 1998). A second strand has involved econometric analysis, such as Abraham and Brock (2003), Revenga (1992) and Grossman (1987), whereby it is empirically tested whether increasing import competition can be a major factor behind declining employment and sluggish real compensation growth in industrialised economies. A third strand has been more eclectic, involving, *inter alia*, general equilibrium models of trade, the analysis of input mixes at the industry level given input mix changes in production as trade is liberalised, and the role of prices (e.g. the evolution of commodity prices over time).

Available empirical evidence has been mixed for what concerns the labour market impact of increasing trade openness. Three main conclusions can be drawn from the extensive review of available literature within OECD (2005) and Molnar *et al.* (2006). First, enhanced trade between developed and developing countries places some downward pressure on the relative returns to unskilled, low-wage workers in developed countries.[2] Second, the direction of causality between trade and employment is not always easy to establish (though several studies report a negative relationship). Third, domestic factors are typically found to be the principal determinant of employment changes.

Available empirical studies have not consistently accounted for the fact that technological progress may have attenuated the impact of increasing trade openness on labour market outcomes, through two key channels.[3] First, trade may also constitute a form of 'technology transfer' – i.e. convergence in technical efficiency within individual countries over time, particularly for trade among developed economies. Second,

---

[2] Further complicating matters, wage adjustment may be more complex in the case of increasingly fragmented production – or 'task-trading' – than it is in the production and exchange of complete goods examined in traditional trade theory. In this context, Grossman and Rossi-Hansberg (2006) argue that, when considering the real wage impacts of offshoring, productivity effects should be considered along with relative price and labour supply effects.

[3] See, for instance, Wood (1994, 1995, 1998), Anderton and Oscarsson (2002) and Thoenig and Verdier (2003).

international competition may lead firms in advanced economies to raise productivity by pursuing 'defensive innovation', including pressure to innovate and/or alter the skill intensity of production in response to a higher degree of trade openness.

A trade-induced technology shock of the type described above can affect the demand for labour either negatively or positively. On the one hand, a positive technology shock may result in higher demand for labour due to scale effects, whilst higher productivity can lead to lower prices, generating further demand for output and labour given associated competitiveness gains (see Amiti and Wei, 2005). On the other hand, higher productivity can translate into job losses, as the same amount of output can be produced with fewer inputs, whilst lower prices for imported inputs can lead to substitution away from domestic labour. Complicating matters further, trade does not have a clear causal effect on productivity. Frictions associated with the adjustment to trade shocks may imply short-term labour market impacts that correlate with productivity, whereby a failure of internal restructuring by domestic companies subject to foreign competition to keep up with any decline in sales may imply falling productivity on the aggregate. At the same time, there may be a composition effect, whereby more productive firms become better exporters.

3   Trade and employment: a factor content of trade analysis

The factor content of trade approach provides quantitative estimates of trade-induced job flows, both in directly affected sectors and in other sectors peripheral to but nonetheless involved in the production process. It assumes a direct link between employment in the sector and output given average output per employee and input-output tables, ascertaining the extent to which labour is used in producing US exports and how much would have been used to produce the imports. The differences between export and import labour content are then interpreted as the impact of trade on the demand for workers, by comparison with what it would have been in the absence of trade.[4] Concerning the export demand effect, the

---

[4] As with any empirical approach, several assumptions are required in making such calculations. In calculating the factor content of trade, the relevant assumptions are that (1) average values in input-output tables reflect marginal values; (2) there exist few differences in skill intensity between non-exporting firms and exporting firms; (3) factor price equalisation holds – implying that countries facing the same wage and rental rates will produce each good using the same capital/labour ratio; (4) there is no domestic wage response to competitive pressures from imports – i.e. changes in the production of goods are assumed to be output shocks that affect employment at existing wages; and (5) there is inelastic consumer demand across imported goods or their higher-priced domestic

specific method used is designed to capture both direct and indirect effects of trade on employment, whereby:

- direct employment effects from any given volume of exports can be calculated from the contemporaneous level of output per employee in each sector; the most disaggregated data on direct output per employee and international trade we have available are the National Bureau of Economic Research (NBER) productivity and NBER trade databases respectively (which are both in four-digit US standard industrial classification; this classification lists 450 manufacturing industries); and
- indirect employment effects can be considered as the outcome from the inputs from all other industries of the economy required to produce each sector's output (available from input-output tables – in order to avoid aggregation bias, sectoral employment generation should be calculated at the most disaggregated level possible); the indirect employment requirements are estimated on the basis of OECD input-output tables, which are available at a three-digit International Standard Industry Classification (ISIC) level, and we convert the employment requirement and international trade data to this classification using the Statistics Canada concordance tables.

As a result, we can estimate for twenty manufacturing industries the direct and indirect employment generated from trade. The employment content of US exports in year t is therefore calculated as

$$LNN_j = D(I - A)^{-1} (XTR_t) \tag{1}$$

where LNN_t denotes the total employment content in the United States' exports in year t. The $(1 \times j)$ vector D denotes the quantity of employment directly used per unit of output in industry j in year t and the $(j \times j)$ matrix A is the input-output matrix of year 1979. Finally, the $(j \times 1)$ vector XTR_t is the export vector of year t.

To calculate the import competition effect, a similar calculation to that for exports above is made for imports, with the assumption that, if this value of imports had been produced in the United States, output per employee would have been the same as the average for the manufacturing output that actually was produced in the country.

The factor content of trade, FCT, can therefore be calculated by using the following equation,

---

equivalents, possibly leading to an overstatement of how much domestic production is displaced by imports (the elasticities and cross-elasticities of product demand for various goods that would be required for such a calculation are not readily available).

$$FCT_j = \sum_t (X_{jt} - M_{jt}) \times \left(\frac{L_{jt}}{Q_{jt}}\right) \qquad (2)$$

where X represents exports, M imports, L employment and Q output, and j is the sector concerned.

With regard to the data underlying the calculations, comprehensive data are available for 1989–2001, while a more limited data set is available for the period 2000–4. In order to obtain a lengthier time series for analysis, calculations are made for the two specific periods given two separate sources and connected together for continuous analysis. The calculations made for the period 1989–2001 make use of comprehensive NBER trade data,[5] while aggregate data over the period 2000–2004 come from the database of the US International Trade Commission.[6,7]

3.1   Aggregate US manufacturing employment

A secular decline in US manufacturing sector employment in conjunction with increased trade openness has been apparent for the last fifteen years. Since 2000 this phenomenon has intensified in parallel with the increasing importance of China in US trade. A geographical breakdown of the United States' trade balance indicates that China comprised the largest bilateral share of the US deficit in goods in 2004, at 25 per cent of the total (compared with 16 per cent for the European Union as a whole).[8] This predominantly reflects strong US imports of goods from China – amounting to a 16 per cent share in 2004 – while bilateral goods exports from the United States to China amounted to only 4 per cent of total goods exports. Within the manufacturing sector (i.e. excluding other components of the goods sector, such as natural resources, mining and

---

[5] Given that relevant data are available only until 1998, an assumption of constant employment requirements must be made from 1998 onwards, thereby imbuing some bias in the case of a systematic impact of technological change on employment requirements over the period of analysis. In addition, in order to maintain consistency with exports expressed in current-year dollars, output per employee is also based on current dollar output.

[6] To compute a current dollar value of output per employee in 2004, we extrapolate the trend rate of price change based on the experience of the five preceding years.

[7] Note that for China, much more than for other US trading partners, there exist significant potential sources of distortion in measuring the value of goods traded with the United States given the centrally planned nature of the Chinese economy. We have elected to rely on US data when making estimates for the impact of Chinese trade on US job creation, as they are more readily available and as the direction of any statistical shortcomings in the trade data is not fully clear.

[8] By 2004 seven countries/territories in east Asia (China, Hong Kong SAR, South Korea, Malaysia, Singapore, Taiwan and Thailand), together with Brazil and Mexico, accounted for 35 per cent of total US manufacturing trade.

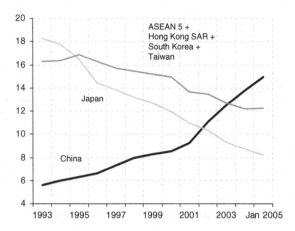

Figure 6.2 US total import shares
(a) US total import shares by economic area

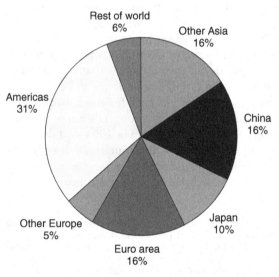

Figure 6.2 (b) US manufacturing import shares by geographical area (2004)

construction), US bilateral manufacturing imports from China increased over the last decade more than twofold (figure 6.2). While this partly reflects the replacement of domestic production with imports from China, it also reflects the displacement of imports from other Asian countries, most notably Japan – with bilateral US imports from China also reflecting the net balance of trade in goods with many Asian

Table 6.1 *Labour content of total goods and manufacturing trade (2000–4) (millions of units unless denoted otherwise)*

	2000	2001	2002	2003	2004	2000–4
Total trade in goods						
Exports ($ billion)	780	731	693	724	817	36
Employment effect – exports	9.91	9.03	8.19	8.11	9.15	−0.76
Imports ($ billion)	1,217	1,142	1,164	1,259	1,470	253
Employment effect – imports	14.46	13.78	13	12.85	15	0.54
Net employment effect	−4.55	−4.75	−4.81	−4.74	−5.84	−1.3
Manufacturing trade						
Exports ($ billion)	707	656	622	645	727	19
Employment effect of exports	8.98	8.11	7.35	7.23	8.15	−0.84
Imports ($ billion)	1,024	961	985	1,048	1,214	190
Employment effect of imports	12.17	11.59	11	10.69	12.39	0.21
Net employment effects	−3.19	−3.48	−3.65	−3.46	−4.24	−1.05

Sources: US International Trade Commission database and authors' calculations.

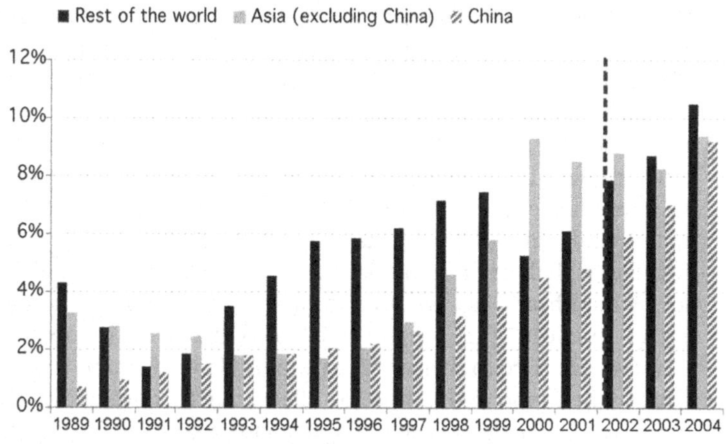

Figure 6.3 Labour content of US goods trade with China and the rest of the world relative to total manufacturing employment

countries that is channelled primarily through China, manufacturers having shifted the final assembly of many of their products from other Asian countries (and perhaps a few non-Asian countries) to China (see Holtz-Eakin, 2005).

Factor content of trade calculations indicate that the labour content of US trade increased from less than 20 per cent of total US manufacturing employment in 1999 to nearly 30 per cent in 2004. For 2004 the net job migration associated with net manufacturing trade was more or less equally split between China, the rest of Asia and the rest of the world, so that job flows to each area associated with trade totalled roughly 10 per cent of total manufacturing employment in that year (see figure 6.3). This implies that the jobs displaced in 2004 by the net import of manufactured goods into the United States accounted for just below one-third of total manufacturing employment, which contrasts starkly with the situation in the early 1990s, when the job content of net manufacturing trade was equal to 10 per cent of total US manufacturing employment per annum.

In examining developments since 2000 in more detail (see table 6.1), it would appear that both export weakness – in conjunction with domestic productivity improvements – and strength in imports have both contributed to international job outflows from the US manufacturing sector.

- On the export side, in 2000 $780 billion US total goods exports are estimated to have generated almost 10 million jobs. By 2004, while exports had risen to $817 billion, only 9 million jobs were required to produce the export goods in that year. Indeed, as shown in the last column in the table, a net rise in the dollar value of exports over the 2000–4 period actually led to an estimated net decrease of job requirements of around three-quarters of a million units – indicating that strong US labour productivity growth implied that fewer workers were required in 2004 to produce the same output as in 2000.
- On the import side, in 2000 $1,217 billion US total goods imports would have required between around 14.5 million workers if these imports had been produced in the United States, given the US productivity level at that time. By 2004 US imports had risen to $1,470 billion, which, taken together with the increase in productivity, implies that around 15 million jobs would have been required to produce these imports in the United States – indicating that a net rise in the dollar value of imports over the 2000–4 period led to an increase of imported jobs of around half a million.
- Taking the export and import job effects together, we find that between 2000 and 2004 in total the labour content of trade had increased by 1.3 million jobs. When narrowing the focus to only manufacturing, table 6.2 shows that around 80 per cent of the increased labour content of trade between 2000 and 2004 can be ascribed to manufacturing trade, and in particularly to the rise in manufacturing imports. It should be noted, however, that the bulk of the changes actually occurred in 2004, given a 780,000 job increase in the labour content of trade in that year.[9]

---

[9] These results are broadly in line with Bronfenbrenner and Luce (2004) for the 2000–3 period but exceed the numbers detected in their findings for 2004, when about 75–80 per cent of the jobs were lost in the manufacturing sector.

Table 6.2 *The role of trade in the recent US 'jobless recovery'* *(2000–3) (percentage change)*

	Total employment	of which: net trade	of which: domestic use
Total employment	−1.36	−0.14	−1.22
Manufacturing employment	−15.97	−1.59	−14.39

Note: Domestic use is calculated as the residual.

Source: Authors' calculations.

To put these magnitudes into perspective, one can assess the extent to which the weakness in US employment between 2000 and 2003 – often dubbed the 'jobless recovery' – is due to trade and other (interpreted as domestic) factors. The change in the share of trade in total employment and manufacturing employment over the 2000–3 period indicates that domestic factors clearly outweigh international ones for both total and manufacturing employment (see table 6.2).

In calculating a geographical breakdown of net manufacturing job flows stemming from trade, regional reallocations of production appear to have been important over the 2000–4 period. In particular, China is becoming more important in relative terms, whereas Asia excluding China is becoming less so (see figure 6.4). This is the case not just for total trade but, even more clearly, for manufacturing trade, in which around 50 per cent of the total increase in the labour content of trade derives from bilateral trade with China. As a result of trade with China, 635,000 more jobs were 'net-traded' between 2000 and 2004, most of which were in manufacturing. At the same time, however, the labour content of trade in the United States decreased thanks to trade with Asia, namely by around 335,000 jobs, again most of which were in manufacturing. This indicates that it is in fact most likely that the jobs currently described in the United States as being 'imported' from China had already been imported before and (probably from Asia excluding China).[10]

---

[10] This is consistent with Eichengreen *et al.* (2004), who find that Chinese exports crowd out those from other Asian countries. These results also confirm the findings of the Hong Kong Monetary Authority (2004), which argues that, in 2004, 56 per cent of intra-regional trade within non-Japan Asia was related to processing trade – as around 48 per cent of China's imports from non-Japan Asia are intended to meet the input demand of its exporting industries.

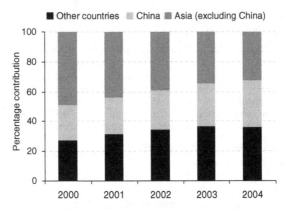

Figure 6.4 Relative importance of Asia (excluding China) and China job content of goods trade
(a) Manufacturing job content of goods trade

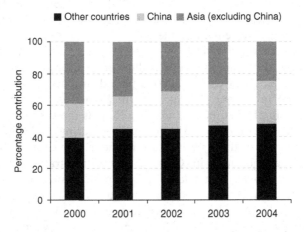

Figure 6.4 (b) Total economy job content of goods trade

3.2   *Sectoral US manufacturing employment*

The decline in US manufacturing employment arising from trade, in particular during the most recent period, appears to have been most concentrated in low-skilled sectors (see figure 6.5). Between 1989 and 2000 the largest source of net estimated job destruction arising from trade appears to have been textiles, followed by metal-producing sectors, 'manufacturing not elsewhere classified (n.e.c.) – recycling' (which includes, *inter alia*, jewellery, musical instruments, toys and stationery) and 'radio, television and communication equipment'. China's role in the

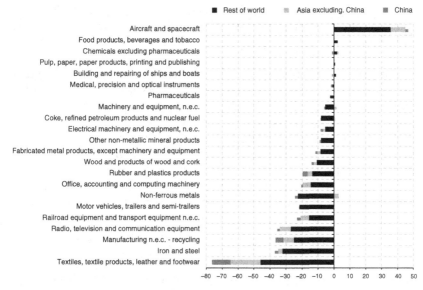

Figure 6.5 Labour content of trade (1989–2000)

latter development appears to have been most pronounced in textile production, followed by 'manufacturing n.e.c. – recycling'. In contrast, the net trade impact on US employment was strongly positive for the highly specialised area of aircraft and spacecraft production.

4 Impacts of increasing openness by region on the labour market: a sectoral VAR analysis

In this section, we complement the analysis of the previous section by considering the impacts of trade on other variables as well as employment, notably wages and productivity. The framework employed is based on the sectoral VAR model applied by Hiebert and Vansteenkiste (2008), which is a direct application of the global VAR of Dees *et al.* (2007) from a multi-country to a multi-sector setting, refined to examine the impact of trade flows *by region*. In particular, trade flows are analysed with respect to three regions: emerging markets, developed economies (termed here as 'rest of the world') and NAFTA members.[11] While the first two

---

[11] The NAFTA economies, in addition to the United States, are Canada and Mexico. Emerging market economies are comprised of Asia excluding Japan and Latin America excluding Mexico. 'Rest of world' includes the euro area, the United Kingdom, Australia, New Zealand, Japan, Hong Kong SAR and South Korea.

country groupings (broadly, emerging versus developed economies) offer some insights into the differential labour market impacts of trade, the third grouping (NAFTA) gives some further perspective on the role of regionalisation.

The sectoral VAR analysis is complementary to the factor content calculations insofar as it provides a richer assessment of labour market outcomes in a holistic context, allowing for interactions between industry employment, wages, productivity and the capital stock, along with an analysis of all manufacturing trade, not just goods that are traded internationally. This comes at the cost, however, of a less fine regional focus in examining impacts.

Below, we briefly describe general aspects of the sectoral VAR model, then analyse the impulse responses yielded by such a framework.

4.1   *The sectoral VAR model*

The sectoral VAR model explicitly allows for interdependencies that exist between sectoral and manufacturing-wide factors, thereby enabling an analysis of the industry effects of exogenous common or sector-specific shocks, as well as an assessment of spillovers from industry-specific shocks to endogenous variables within the system.[12]

For each industry N, we assume that industry-specific variables, x, are related to corresponding industry-specific weighted averages of the same variable in all other industries, x^*, along with deterministic variables, such as a time trend, t, and weakly exogenous variables, dt. In a first-order dynamic specification, we can then relate industry-specific variables to industry-wide exogenous variables and write

$$x_{it} = a_{io} + a_{i1}t + \Phi_i x_{i,t-1} + \Lambda_{i0} x_{i,t}^* + \Lambda_{i1} x_{i,t-1}^* + \psi_{i0} d_t + \psi_{i1} d_{t-1} + \mu_{i0} m_t + \mu_{i1} m_{t-1} + \varepsilon_{it}$$

where Φ_i is a $k_i \times k_i$ matrix of lagged coefficients, Λ_{i0} and Λ_{i1} are $k_i \times k_i^*$ matrices of coefficients associated with the industry-specific variables, ψ_{i0} and ψ_{i1} are $ki \times s$ matrices of coefficients associated with the common industry-wide variables and ε_{it} is a $k_i \times 1$ vector of idiosyncratic industry-specific shocks. We assume that the industry-specific variance-covariance matrices are time-invariant, which for the analysis of annual observations

---

[12] This framework is therefore a sectoral analogue of the multi-country sectoral VAR of Dees *et al.* (2007), examining *sector-specific* rather than *country-specific* shocks and spillovers.

is not overly restrictive, and treat dt and x_{it}^* as weakly exogenous $I(1)$ with respect to the parameters of this model.

This weak exogeneity assumption in the context of cointegrating models implies no long-run feedbacks from x_{it} to x_{it}^*, without necessarily ruling out lagged short-run feedbacks between the two sets of variables. We estimate the parameters of the cross-section-specific models separately, treating the industry-specific averages of variables in all other industries as weakly exogenous on the grounds that industries are small relative to the size of the overall manufacturing sector, to provide a complete system. Overall, the manufacturing-wide model associated with the industry-specific models can now be given by

$$Gx_t = a_0 + a_1 t + Hx_{i,t-1} + \psi_0 d_t + \psi_1 d_{t-1} + \mu_0 m_t + \mu_1 m_{t-1} + \varepsilon_t$$

where $a_0, a_1, \psi_0, \psi_1, \mu_0, \mu_1, G, H$ and ε_t can be defined as $(j = 0$ or $1)$

$$a_j = \begin{pmatrix} a_{oj} \\ a_{1j} \\ \dots \\ a_{Nj} \end{pmatrix} \varepsilon_t = \begin{pmatrix} \varepsilon_{ot} \\ \varepsilon_{1t} \\ \dots \\ \varepsilon_{Nt} \end{pmatrix} \psi/\mu_j = \begin{pmatrix} \psi/\mu_{oj} \\ \psi/\mu_{1j} \\ \dots \\ \psi/\mu_{Nj} \end{pmatrix} G = \begin{pmatrix} A_0 W_0 \\ A_1 W_1 \\ \dots \\ A_N W_N \end{pmatrix} H = \begin{pmatrix} B_0 W_0 \\ B_1 W_1 \\ \dots \\ B_N W_N \end{pmatrix}$$

whereby Wi is a $(k_i \times k_i^*) \times k$ matrix of fixed constants defined in terms of the state-specific weights. W_i can be viewed as the link matrix that allows the state-specific models to be written in terms of the global variable vector x_t.

We analysed twelve US manufacturing sectors classified according to the ISIC revision 3.[13] The frequency is annual, and spans the period 1977–2003 (i.e. a T dimension of twenty-five and an N dimension of twelve). The endogenous sector-specific variables, xit, included in the model are real compensation per employee (*COMP*), productivity (*PROD*), full-time equivalent employment (*EMPL*) and the capital stock (*CAP*). For each sector we assume that the sector-specific variables are related to an exogenous sector-specific variable (namely trade openness, measured as the sum of exports and imports of goods by sector) and manufacturing-wide variables (measured as a sector-specific weighted average of the other sectors – henceforth star variables, x_{it}^*). A set of deterministic variables, such as time trends (t), is also included, along

---

[13] A thirteenth sector under the ISIC classification, 'coke, refined petroleum products and nuclear fuel', was excluded on the grounds that factors autonomous from those affecting other industries probably drive its evolution relative to the other sectors.

with common manufacturing-wide (weakly) exogenous variables (d_t), consisting of trade openness $(OPEN)$. The sources and the construction of the data are discussed in more detail in appendix B.

4.2   The sectoral VAR results

In this section, we analyse generalised impulse response functions (GIRFs) of employment, real compensation and productivity to shocks to trade openness by region, for (1) emerging markets, (2) NAFTA economies and (3) the rest of the world.[14] Impulse responses are presented for twenty years following the imposition of a shock.

Figure 6.6 displays the average, maximum and minimum of sectoral bootstrap estimates of GIRFs for the four endogenous variables of the sectoral VAR system, while figure 6.7 presents the sectoral impacts of shocks to trade with each of the above three regions. A one standard error positive shock results in a one percentage point increase in US manufacturing trade openness with these economies.

4.2.1   Employment The impulse responses indicate that increased trade openness exerts almost no impact on the full-time equivalent employment when averaging across all sectors of US manufacturing, independent of the region of origin of trade (see figure 6.6a). While the average industry employment response is initially mildly negative for trade with emerging market economies, mildly positive for trade with developed economies, the long-run response is essentially zero. That said, the range of industry responses varies widely, with trade with NAFTA and emerging market economies exhibiting a somewhat higher range of industry employment responses than is the case with trade with developed economies. Such heterogeneity could be related to a higher use of offshoring to regions with lower costs, either in the form of labour (emerging markets) or transaction costs associated with trade (NAFTA).

In general, trade openness has a positive impact on employment, while employment in secondary manufacturing industries tends to exhibit a more mixed response (see figure 6.7a).[15] The 'mineral products' category

---

[14] The GIRF approach considers shocks to individual errors and integrates out the effects of the other shocks using the observed distribution of all the shocks without any orthogonalisation. In this way, it is invariant to the ordering of variables and sectors.

[15] *Primary* manufacturing industries are assumed to be those that rely to a great extent on the processing of natural resources from agriculture, fishing, forestry or mining – i.e. (1) food products, (2) wood, (3) paper products, (4) non-metallic minerals, (5) basic metals and (6) non-metallic mineral products. *Secondary* manufacturing industries are assumed to be

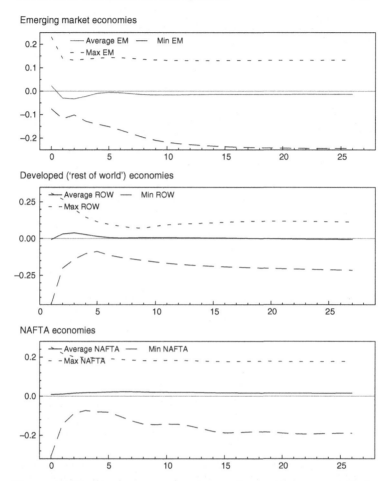

Figure 6.6 Impulse responses by region of a positive one standard deviation shock to US manufacturing trade openness
(a) Impact on full-time equivalent employment

generally displays the largest positive employment responses to trade openness in the long run, particularly related to trade with NAFTA economies. A large positive employment response is also evident for openness in 'other transport equipment' with respect to other developed economies, where it is conceivable that the airline industry (representing the bulk of 'other transport') benefits quickly from trade though some gains

those that have less direct links to natural resources – i.e. (1) textiles, (2) chemical products, (3) fabricated metal products, (4) machinery and equipment, (5) motor vehicles and (6) other transport equipment.

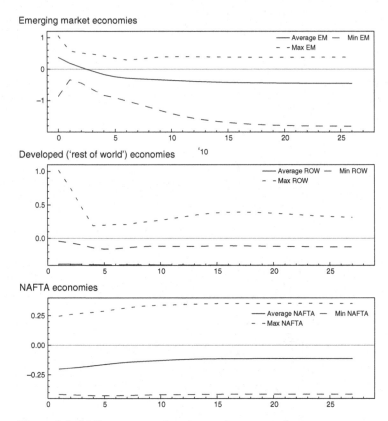

Figure 6.6 (b) Impact on real compensation per employee

erode with time given competition. The largest employment losses result-ing from trade openness over the long run appear to emanate from 'textiles' and 'fabricated metals'. It is notable that NAFTA economies appear to have a markedly different from average profile for 'wood products', a sector affected by Canada–US trade disputes, and 'textiles'.

The dynamics of the system, whereby the initial impacts are generally larger and the effect of the shock decays through time, could be consistent with several factors, including adjustment costs in reallocating labour, frictions in varying the intensity of the labour workforce in particular sectors and a gradual loss of market share when faced with competition. Moreover, capital/labour substitution, particularly in connection with technology transfer associated with trade, may impart some equilibrium shifts, as well as persistence in the adjustment dynamics of employment to changes in openness.

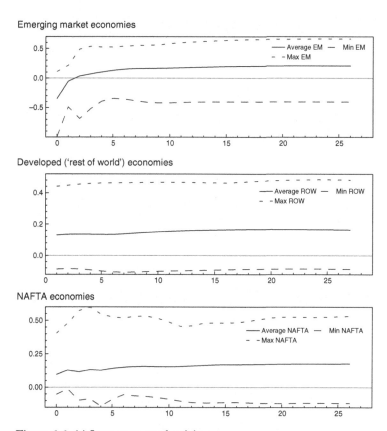

Figure 6.6 (c) Impact on productivity

4.2.2   Real compensation In theory, developments in real compensation are likely to differ across industries because specialisation based on domestic factor endowments relative to the factor endowments of trading partners differs. One concrete possibility is that improved communications may have allowed large firms to fragment their operations, moving more unskilled-labour-intensive stages of production to countries where unskilled wages are low, so lowering unskilled wages in developed countries while simultaneously raising skilled wages in developing countries (see, for instance, Neary, 2005). Moreover, the duration of the shock may be of importance. In this context, Terfous (2006) contrasts a temporary adjustment effect on developed economies' labour markets (given frictions in related adjustment) with lasting effects (through changing the skill composition of the demand for labour and trade-induced technical progress).

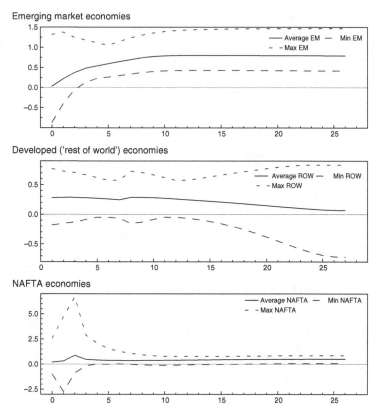

Figure 6.6 (d) Impact on capital stock

The impulse responses from a shock to openness by region indicate that increased trade openness exerts a negative impact on real compensation when averaging across all sectors of US manufacturing, with a proportionately larger fall in wages resulting from trade openness with emerging market economies in the medium to long run (see figure 6.6b). The latter finding could very well correspond to the cost differential between the United States and emerging market trading partners (obviously less present in developed economy trading partners), and an associated compression of wages deriving from competition and outsourcing, or even the threat of such developments. The range of wage outcomes is also broadest for emerging market economies. The wage response of trade openness appears to be broadly consistent concerning NAFTA economies and developed ('rest of the world') economies, to a much larger extent than with employment as reported in the above

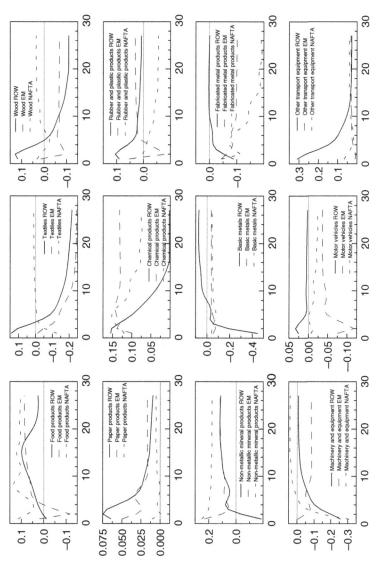

Figure 6.7 Summary of impulse responses by sector of a positive one standard deviation shock to US manufacturing trade openness by region

(a) Impact on full-time equivalent employment

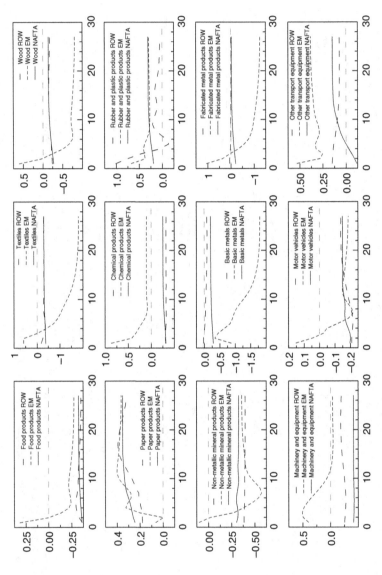

Figure 6.7 (b) Impact on real compensation per employee

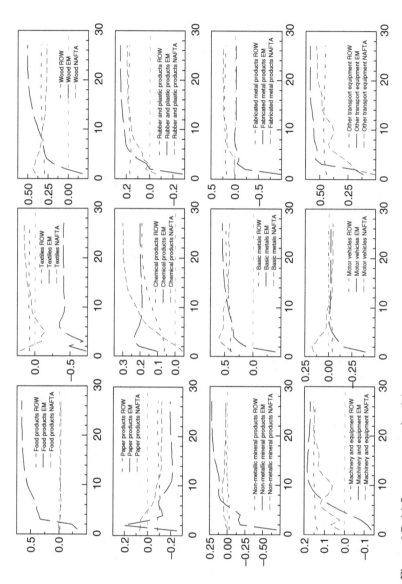

Figure 6.7 (c) Impact on productivity

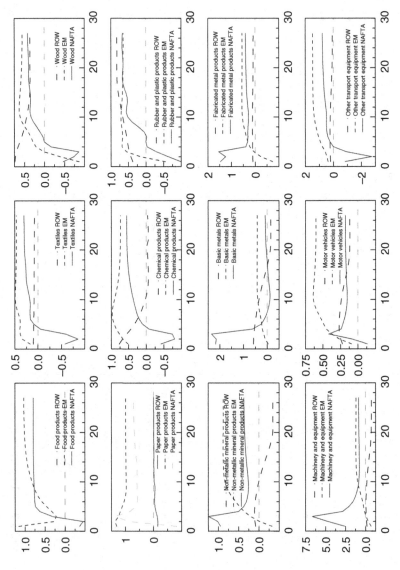

Figure 6.7 (d) Impact on capital stock

subsection, possibly signalling the importance of initial conditions in wage convergence.

In general, wages in secondary industries appear to be more negatively affected than those in primary industries (see figure 6.7b). Compensation for labour in 'textiles', for instance, is affected strongly by increased openness with emerging market and developed economies, a feature also shared by the 'fabricated metal products' sector in connection with trade with NAFTA economies. It would seem that the comparative advantage of skill bias may be playing some role in wage developments, with 'other transport equipment', 'rubber and plastic products' and 'paper products' all registering positive wage responses to industry openness.

The dynamics of the system indicate a drop in wages followed by a gradual improvement, on average, concerning trade with NAFTA, while there is some worsening of wages over time in connection with trade with emerging market economies and other developed economies. Interestingly, the average industry employment response is initially positive for trade with emerging market economies, then becomes negative with time – possibly corresponding to some downward wage rigidities. Such developments could be in keeping with the difference between trade governed by bilateral agreements and other trade, with the former possibly suggesting a gradual enhancement of integration and trading possibilities with RTAs, in contrast to the latter suggesting some possible loss of market share when faced with competition.

4.2.3 Productivity Several studies point to a positive productivity impact of increased trade openness, given international technology transfer or defensive innovation on the part of import-competing firms. Lawrence (2000) finds that import competition has a positive impact on US total factor productivity, mainly in skill-intensive sectors and industries competing with developing countries. This may derive from defensive innovation and it may also reflect firm composition, whereby, in response to greater foreign competition, profit margins fall as mark-ups decline and average productivity rises as marginal firms exit the industry (see also Chen *et al.*, 2004). In distinguishing any correlation of productivity with openness into a causal relationship, both directions of causality are possible. On the one hand, frictions associated with the adjustment to trade shocks may imply short-term labour market impacts that correlate with productivity. In particular, domestic companies subject to foreign competition may pursue internal restructuring involving lay-offs and firm closures – though, if such restructuring does not keep up with the decline in sales, which is plausible given adjustment costs in the intensity of employment along with hiring and firing costs, this may imply falling productivity on the aggregate. Bernard *et al.* (2006) find that plant survival and growth are negatively associated with industry exposure to low-wage country imports. On the other hand, the causality may go in the other direction due to a composition effect, whereby more productive firms become better exporters.

Impulse responses from a shock to openness by region indicate that increased trade openness appears to exert a positive impact on productivity when averaging across all sectors of US manufacturing, regardless of the regional orientation to openness (see figure 6.6c). Moreover, this average positive productivity effect appears to grow slightly over time. When comparing between regions, it appears that the increase in average industry productivity as a result of trade is largest for trade with emerging market economies, but it occurs only with a lag as it is only after some years that the initial negative responses become positive and larger than those prompted by trade with both NAFTA partners and other developed economies.

Productivity is positively affected by openness in both primary and secondary industries alike, with the only notable exceptions of 'paper products', 'motor vehicles' and 'textiles' (see figure 6.7c). The largest boost to productivity appears to be present in 'other transport equipment', 'fabricated metals', 'food products' and 'basic metals'.

4.2.4   Capital stock The impulse responses from a shock to openness by region indicate that increased trade openness appears to exert a positive impact on the capital stock when averaging across all sectors of US manufacturing, with the largest increases in trade with NAFTA economies (see figure 6.6d). Such an outcome is heavily influenced by a large increase in the capital stock of machinery and equipment, particularly given openness with respect to NAFTA economies and emerging markets.

The magnitude of response in the capital stock appears to be higher in primary than in secondary industries (see figure 6.7d), which is not surprising, on account of the lower raw material content of production and likely higher capital content.

5   Conclusions

This chapter has assessed the extent to which increased trade openness by region has affected labour conditions in advanced economies through an analysis of the US manufacturing sector, on the basis of two separate but complementary methodologies. The first methodology assesses the employment consequences of trade openness on the basis of factor content calculations with a detailed country and sectoral analysis, while the second methodology assesses shocks to openness on the basis of an econometric sectoral VAR methodology that analyses employment, wages and productivity in a cohesive and consistent framework.

Three main conclusions can be drawn regarding the joint impact of trade and structural changes in productivity on labour market outcomes in the manufacturing sector based on these methodologies. First, while a secular decrease in US manufacturing sector employment in conjunction with trade has been apparent for the last two decades, such a decrease appears to have intensified in recent years. Such trade effects appear to be small, however, compared with overall job flows – consistent with most existing literature, which has found that predominantly domestic factors such as skill-biased technical change have been more important than trade factors in explaining manufacturing job flows in the United States (although it should be noted that factor content estimates do not fully account for the probable technology-induced indirect effects of trade on employment). A regional breakdown of trade in the sectoral VAR framework, which captures endogenous productivity responses to trade shocks by region, indicates that higher import competition appears to have manifested itself through real wage rather than employment adjustment in the US manufacturing sector.[16] Second, while the role of China in US trade is increasing sharply, it seems that this is occurring to a large extent at the expense of other Asian countries. Interestingly, trade with NAFTA economies appears to have yielded generally similar labour market, productivity and capital stock outcomes. Third, higher trade openness has mostly affected employment in the lower-skilled manufacturing sectors. This latter finding is consistent with Jaumotte and Tytell (2007), who find that, while the ongoing globalisation of labour has contributed to rising labour compensation in advanced economies by boosting productivity and output, labour compensation has been sluggish in unskilled sectors (even though the latter derives in large part from skill-biased technological change).

These findings indicate that, while growth in international trade would be expected to be welfare-enhancing in the long run through higher living standards and pecuniary gains from specialisation, it may embed some adjustment costs related to distributional effects associated with the sectoral real location of labour. Such wage adjustments may be greater in connection with trade with emerging market economies given the initial

---

[16] The finding of an initial negative impact on labour compensation is consistent with the findings in OECD (2005), where it is reported that large wage losses on the post-displacement job are a particularly important source of post-displacement earnings losses in the United States. The findings of Feenstra (2007) are more nuanced, indicating a fall in real wages of production workers in the US manufacturing sector between the mid-1980s and the mid-1990s, contrasting with a recovery in the latter part of the 1990s and into the current millennium.

wage conditions and an associated compression of wages deriving from competition and outsourcing, or even the threat of such developments. This contrasts with a mild but steady improvement in average industry wages on the basis of the NAFTA regional trade agreement, possibly suggesting that workers gain from trade only after some time has elapsed, given the frictions in industry adjustment.

It should be noted that the analysis in this chapter is partial and the findings restricted to the manufacturing sector. While this chapter has analysed the labour market effects of trade by region in the manufacturing sector, other sectors such as services (for which there are fewer data available) would need to be taken into account in order to develop an accurate picture of trade impacts in the aggregate, as the sectors may have experienced very different impacts from trade.

Appendices

A   *Sectors covered*

ISIC code	Industry name
15–16	Food products, beverages and tobacco
17–19	Textiles, textile products, leather and footwear
20	Wood and products of wood and cork
21–2	Pulp, paper, paper products, printing and publishing
23	Coke, refined petroleum products and nuclear fuel*
24	Chemicals and chemical products
25	Rubber and plastics products
26	Other non-metallic mineral products
27	Basic metals
28	Fabricated metal products, except machinery and equipment
29–33	Machinery and equipment
34	Motor vehicles, trailers and semi-trailers
35	Other transport equipment

*Not included in analysis (see footnote 13).

B   *Data*

Productivity
Definition: Value added per worker.
Units: Index, 2000 = 100; value added divided by employment series (see definition below).

Sources: OECD STructural ANalysis (STAN) database for industrial analysis, Bureau of Economic Analysis and Bureau of Labor Statistics.

Employment
Definition: Total employees – full-time equivalent.
Units: Thousands of units.
Source: OECD STAN database for industrial analysis.

Exports
Definition: Exports of goods.
Units: Index, 2000 = 100; current price export series are measured in millions of dollars and deflated using value added in current and constant prices per industry.
Sources: OECD STAN database for industrial analysis and Bureau of Economic Analysis.

Imports
Definition: Imports of goods.
Units: Index, 2000 = 100; current price import series are measured in millions of dollars and deflated with the aid of value added in current and constant prices per industry.
Sources: OECD STAN database for industrial analysis and Bureau of Economic Analysis.

Openness
Definition: Sum of exports and imports of goods by sector.
Units: Index (see exports and imports).
Sources: OECD STAN database for industrial analysis and Bureau of Economic Analysis.

Oil
Definition: West Texas Intermediate spot price deflated using the price index for personal consumption expenditures.
Units: Dollars expressed in 2000 quarter 1 prices.
Sources: Dow Jones & Company (oil price) and Bureau of Economic Analysis (price deflator).

Compensation
Definition: Wages and salaries of employees paid by producers, as well as supplements such as contributions to social security, private pensions, health insurance, life insurance and similar schemes.
Units: Index, 2000 = 100; nominal series are measured in millions of dollars and deflated with the aid of value added in current and constant prices per industry.

Sources: OECD STAN database for industrial analysis and Bureau of Labor Statistics.

Research and development spending
Definition: Analytical Business Enterprise Research and Development.
Units: Millions of dollars.
Sources: OECD Research and Development Expenditure in Industry database.

Capital stock
Definition: Initial capital stock calculated for 1975; for the years following investment series are accumulated and depreciated.
Sources: OECD STAN database for industrial analysis and Bureau of Economic Analysis.
Calculation: (see Griliches, 1979)

$$K_{1978} = I_{1978} + (1 - \delta)\lambda I_{1978} + (1 - \delta)^2\lambda^2 I_{1978} + \ldots$$

$$= I_{1978}\left(\frac{1}{1 - \lambda(1 - \delta)}\right)$$

where $\lambda = \frac{1}{1+\eta}$ and η is the mean annual growth rate of investments over the period 1970–8. The depreciation rate δ is set to equal 13.33 per cent.

C   *Aggregation weights*

See table 6A.1.

Table 6A.1 *Input-output table implied weights*

	15–16	17–19	20	21–2	24	25	26	27	28	29–33	34	35
15–16	0.00	10.43	2.93	5.46	5.14	1.13	1.23	1.01	0.57	4.48	0.50	0.50
17–19	1.84	0.00	3.64	15.89	3.12	6.62	2.75	0.94	0.63	6.33	4.54	1.89
20	2.43	3.46	0.00	14.35	2.23	1.09	3.59	2.57	1.12	8.05	1.08	0.87
21–2	23.75	23.60	7.82	0.00	21.19	9.36	17.80	7.02	4.97	43.87	4.07	3.46
24	21.59	3.61	20.12	1.15	0.00	57.19	25.41	12.28	9.18	0.71	8.98	7.67
25	12.86	21.57	7.58	0.70	17.04	0.00	7.79	4.68	3.34	0.61	8.80	5.07
26	4.73	4.06	7.52	0.03	4.18	2.52	0.00	10.03	2.53	0.04	2.99	1.77
27	5.49	0.08	7.51	0.49	7.28	4.17	10.15	0.00	60.78	4.12	27.20	16.97
28	13.16	0.58	16.77	25.95	14.40	5.77	10.62	24.90	0.00	8.23	16.61	20.85
29–33	10.74	28.64	19.52	31.34	21.73	10.54	15.94	31.81	14.34	0.00	24.84	38.38
34	2.91	3.95	6.03	4.63	3.10	1.37	4.06	3.86	2.22	23.53	0.00	2.57
35	0.51	0.02	0.58	0.02	0.59	0.25	0.67	0.90	0.31	0.02	0.39	0.00

Note: Rows and columns correspond to the ISIC revision 3 code of the relevant sector (see appendix A for detail on the sectoral codes).

References

Abraham, F., and E. Brock (2003), 'Sectoral Employment Effects of Trade and Productivity in the Europe', *Applied Economics*, **35**, 2, 223–38.

Amiti, M., and S.-J. Wei (2005), 'Service Offshoring, Productivity, and Employment: Evidence from the United States', Working Paper no. 05/238, International Monetary Fund, Washington, DC.

Anderton, R., and S. Oscarsson (2002), 'Inequality, Trade and Defensive Innovation in the USA', Research Paper no. 2002/28, Leverhulme Centre for Research on Globalisation and Economic Policy, University of Nottingham.

Baily, M., and R. Z. Lawrence (2004), 'What Happened to the Great US Job Machine? The Role of Trade and Electronic Offshoring', *Brookings Papers on Economic Activity*, **2**:2004, 211–84.

Bernard, A. B., J. B. Jensen and P. K. Schott (2006), 'Survival of the Best Fit: Exposure to Low-wage Countries and the (Uneven) Growth of US Manufacturing Plants', *Journal of International Economics*, **68**, 1, 219–37.

Bhagwati, J. (1998), 'Play It Again, Sam: A New Look at Trade and Wages', mimeo, Columbia University, New York.

Bronfenbrenner, K., and S. Luce (2004), 'The Changing Nature of Corporate Global Restructuring: The Impact of Production Shifts on Jobs in the US, China, and Around the Globe', submission to the US–China Economic and Security Review Commission, Washington, DC.

Chen, N., J. Imbs and A. Scott (2004), 'Competition, Globalization and the Decline of Inflation', Discussion Paper no. 4695, Centre for Economic Policy Research, London.

Dees, S., F. di Mauro, M. H. Pesaran and L. V. Smith (2007), 'Exploring the International Linkages of the Euro Area: A Global VAR Analysis', *Journal of Applied Econometrics*, **22**, 1, 1–38.

Eichengreen, B., Y. Rhee and H. Tong (2004), 'The Impact of China on the Exports of Other Asian Countries', Working Paper no. 10768, National Bureau of Economic Research, Cambridge, MA.

Feenstra, R. C. (2007), 'Globalization and Its Impact on Labor', Global Economy Lecture, Vienna Institute for International Economic Studies, 8 February.

Griliches, Z. (1979), 'Issues in Assessing the Contribution of Research and Development to Productivity Growth', *Bell Journal of Economics*, **10**, 1, 92–116.

Grossman, G. M. (1987), 'The Employment and Wage Effects of Import Competition in the United States', *Journal of International Economic Integration*, **2**, 1, 1–23.

Grossman, G. M., and E. Rossi-Hansberg (2006), 'The Rise of Offshoring: It's Not Wine for Cloth Anymore', mimeo, Princeton University, NJ.

Hiebert, P., and I. Vansteenkiste (2008), 'International Trade, Technological Shocks and Spillovers in the Labour Market: A GVAR Analysis of the US Manufacturing Sector', *Applied Economics* (forthcoming).

Holtz-Eakin, D. (2005), 'Economic Relationships between the US and China', testimony before the Committee on Ways and Means, US House of Representatives, Washington, DC, 14 April.

Hong Kong Monetary Authority (2004), 'The Impact of a Renminbi Appreciation on Global Imbalances and Intra-regional Trade', *Quarterly Bulletin*, March, 16–26.

Jaumotte, F., and I. Tytell (2007), 'The Globalization of Labor', in *World Economic Outlook* (Spring) (Washington, DC: International Monetary Fund), 161–92.

Lawrence, R. Z. (2000), 'Does a Kick in the Pants Get You Going or Does It Just Hurt? The Impact of International Competition on Technological Change in US Manufacturing', in R. C. Feenstra (ed.), *The Impact of International Trade on Wages* (Chicago: University of Chicago Press), 197–224.

Molnar, M., N. Pain and D. Taglioni (2006), 'The Internationalisation of Production, International Outsourcing and OECD Labour Markets', Working Paper no. 561, Economics Department, Organisation for Economic Co-operation and Development, Paris.

Neary, J. P. (2005), 'The Stolper–Samuelson Theorem', in J. J. McCusker (ed.), *Encyclopedia of World Trade since 1450* (New York: Macmillan), 719–20.

OECD (2005), 'Trade-adjustment Costs in OECD Labour Markets: A Mountain or a Molehill?', in *OECD Employment Outlook* (Paris: Organisation for Economic Co-operation and Development), 23–72.

Revenga, A. L. (1992), 'Exporting Jobs? The Impact of Import Competition on Employment and Wages in US Manufacturing', *Quarterly Journal of Economics*, **107**, 1, 255–84.

Sachs, J. D., and H. Shatz (1994), 'Trade and Jobs in US Manufacturing', *Brookings Papers on Economic Activity*, 1:1994, 1–84.

Terfous, N. (2006), 'Globalization and the Labour Market in the Developed Countries', *Diagnostics Prévisions et Analyses Economiques*, 96.

Thoenig, M., and T. Verdier (2003), 'A Theory of Defensive Skill-biased Innovation and Globalization', *American Economic Review*, **93**, 3, 709–28.

Venables, A. J. (2001), 'International Trade: Economic Integration', in N. J. Smelser and P. B. Baltes (eds.) *International Encyclopedia of the Social and Behavioral Sciences* (Oxford: Pergamon), 7843–8.

Wood, A. (1994), *North–South Trade, Employment and Inequality: Changing Fortunes in a Skill-driven World* (Oxford: Oxford University Press).

(1995), 'How Trade Hurt Unskilled Workers', *Journal of Economic Perspectives*, **9**, 3, 57–80.

(1998), 'Globalisation and the Rise in Labour Market Inequalities', *Economic Journal*, **108**, 1463–82.

Index

Printed in the United States
By Bookmasters